Law and Society in Transition

Toward Responsive Law

Philippe Nonet
Philip Selznick

OCTAGON BOOKS

A DIVISION OF FARRAR, STRAUS AND GIROUX

New York   1978

Published 1978

OCTAGON BOOKS
A DIVISION OF FARRAR, STRAUS & GIROUX, INC.
19 Union Square West
New York, N.Y. 10003

Library of Congress Cataloging in Publication Data

Nonet, Philippe.
  Law and society in transition.

    Includes index.
    1. Sociological jurisprudence. I. Selznick, Philip, 1919-
  joint author. II. Title.
K370.N66   340.1′15   78-9368
ISBN 0-374-96116-6

Manufactured by Braun-Brumfield, Inc.
Ann Arbor, Michigan
Printed in the United States of America

Contents

Preface

The discussions from which this essay emerged began about ten years ago, when, with the support of the Ford Foundation, the Center for the Study of Law and Society undertook to examine the crises of law and authority that were, as it then appeared, eroding the foundations of all our institutions. Viewed from the steps of Sproul Hall on the Berkeley campus, the horizon appeared alternatively darkened by threatening clouds and brightened by promising lights. There emerged a conception of the responsive polity, an idea that captured many legal and social aspirations of the day and was offered as a sharp contrast to the repressive idiom of "law and order."

Time has put those eventful days in perspective, moderating earlier judgments and hopes. But we remain deeply indebted to all the students and colleagues who contributed to the stimulating environment and sometimes frenetic activity that marked the Center in those days. Special thanks are due to Forrest Dill, Caleb Foote, Paul Jacobs, Mortimer R. Kadish, Sanford H. Kadish, David Matza, Sheldon L. Messinger, Peter Miller, C. Michael Otten, Antonie A. G. Peters, Martin Roysher, Jerome H. Skolnick, and Rodney Stark.

We first presented an outline of the argument at a seminar on the sociology of law organized in Oxford by Jean Floud, then of Nuffield College, and Phillip Lewis of All Souls College during the Trinity term of 1971. We are grateful for their generous interest and response, as well as for the hospitality of their colleges during that term. In 1973 Philip Selznick delivered a public lecture on "Modern Society and Responsive Law" at University College, London, and we wish to thank Dennis Lloyd and his colleagues for their cordial reception.

Thereafter the work progressed with exceedingly deliberate speed, moving through successive drafts and revisions, and often interrupted by other obligations and distractions. A preliminary draft provided a framework for several classes in the sociology of law at Berkeley, and we are indebted to the many students who expressed interest in the work and whose criticisms stimulated significant revisions. During those years Robert Bell, Robert A. Kagan, Pamela Utz, Paul van Seters, and Kenneth I. Winston gave generously of their time, thought, and moral support. A nearly final version was presented by Philippe Nonet at the 1976 meeting of the Association of American Law Schools, Section on Jurisprudence; we are grateful to Gray Dorsey, Robert C. L. Moffat, and Alan Stone for their comments on that occasion. Finally, we have benefited from the encouragement and criticism of Abraham Edel, David L. Kirp, Leo Lowenthal, and Aaron Wildavsky.

I

Jurisprudence and Social Science

The past twenty years have seen a strong revival of interest in legal institutions—how they work, the forces that impinge upon them, their limits and potentialities. This revival was, in the first instance, largely limited to the world of scholarship. During the 1950s there was an upsurge of hope that a new social science would redeem the promise of an older generation to explore reasons and remedies for the apparent isolation of the legal order.[1] There had long been a sense that lawmaking, judging, policing, and regulation were all too easily divorced from the realities of social experience and from the ideal of justice itself. The new program reflected both an academic impulse—the extension of social science perspectives and methods of study to the analysis of legal institutions—and

1. In the 1950s the Ford Foundation sponsored a substantial program at the University of Chicago Law School, and in the 1960s the Russell Sage Foundation became a prime mover, supporting more numerous but more modest programs of research and training at a number of universities. The Walter E. Meyer Institute was another important catalyst. The *Law and Society Review* was founded in 1966.

1

a reformist spirit. It was hoped that the time had come when sustained inquiry could yield beneficial results for the administration of justice.

What began as a modest stirring among law professors, social scientists, and foundation officials soon took on a larger significance. The politics of the time placed justice high on the agenda of public concern. Civil rights, poverty, crime, mass protest, urban riots, ecological decay, and the abuse of power gathered unprecedented urgency as social problems. They strained the political community to its limits. The legal order was asked to take on new burdens, find new expedients, and examine its own foundations. Suddenly "law and society" became a topic of the first importance, posing problems far beyond the competence of its votaries to meet or even comprehend.

The complexity of the subject, and the atmosphere of crisis, have produced dissonant voices and one-sided outlooks, each viewing the law from a partial and often partisan perspective. In such a setting it has been difficult to achieve a coherent view of the legal order. Yet intellectual coherence is needed, for the sake of public education as well as for social inquiry. It is important for the citizenry, including the legal profession, to be able to make sense of the troubles of the system, weigh competing values, and develop appropriate expectations. It is important for scholars to appreciate the full range of legal experience, thereby validating and integrating partial perspectives. Without intellectual coherence, there cannot be a rational agenda for social inquiry.

This essay is one attempt to meet the challenge of synthesis. A synthesis can be achieved, we believe, if the study of legal experience rediscovers its continuity with the intellectual concerns of classical jurisprudence. Jurisprudence has always been more than an arcane intellectual discipline. Abstract concepts, such as legal obligation, speak to issues that make a difference for the way law is conceived and how it is used.[2] Philosophical standpoints (such as the critique of positivism) and analytical puzzles (such as the distinction between rule and principle)[3] are implicit schemes for diagnosing the troubles that beset a legal order. Thus legal theory is neither innocent of social consequence nor immune to social influence. Where we look for the foundations of law, the sense we make of the legal process, and the place we give law in society—all profoundly affect the shape of the political community and the reach of social aspirations.

There is a need, we think, to make these implicit concerns more central in jurisprudential inquiry, to encourage a renewed appreciation of the interplay of legal theory and social policy. By policy we have in mind not detailed prescriptions but basic perspectives that determine how public purposes are defined and how practical alternatives are perceived. Jurisprudence gains focus and depth when it self-consciously considers the implications it has for action and institutional design. Philosophical analysis, in turn, helps ensure that basic issues of policy are closely examined, not buried under unscrutinized assumptions and perspectives.

To make jurisprudence more relevant and more alive, there must be a reintegration of legal, political, and social theory. As a step in this direction, we have attempted to recast jurisprudential issues in a social-science perspective. Thus understood, competing philosophical theories are seen as reflecting varieties of legal and social experience. We propose a framework for comparing these experiences, for analyzing the

2. On the relation between concepts of legal obligation and conceptions of law, see Mortimer R. Kadish and Sanford H. Kadish, *Discretion to Disobey: A Study of Lawful Departures from Legal Rules* (Stanford, Ca.: Stanford University Press, 1973), esp. pp. 184–201.
3. See, esp., Ronald Dworkin, "The Model of Rules," *University of Chicago Law Review* 35 (1967): 14; and Graham Hughes, "Rules, Policy and Decision-Making," *Yale Law Journal* 77 (1968): 411.

premises and assessing the worth of alternative modes of legal ordering.

Legal Theory and the Crisis of Authority

As a starting point, we should recall that, characteristically, legal theories are built upon implicit theories of authority. Many concerns and controversies of contemporary jurisprudence have their roots in the crisis of authority that has shaken public institutions.

A mood of diminished confidence in law pervades recent writings.[4] Critics of law have always pointed to its inadequacy as a way of ministering to change and achieving substantive justice. Those anxieties remain, but today a new note is struck by repeated references to a crisis of legitimacy. Conservative alarm over the erosion of authority, the abuses of legal activism, and the breakdown of "law and order" is echoed in a renewed radical attack that stresses the impotence and corruption of the legal order. In this neo-marxist critique two themes predominate. First, legal institutions are said to be inherently tainted, sharing the deficiencies of the social order as a whole and serving primarily as instruments of domination. Here the all-too-evident bias of the law, favoring the haves and shortchanging the have-nots, is cited as decisive evidence. Second, there is an attack on "liberal legalism" itself, on the idea that the ends of justice *can* be served by a purportedly detached, impartial, autonomous system of rules and procedures. These themes involve each other, for "the rule of

4. This crisis of confidence is perhaps most sharply revealed in two recent collections of essays: Eugene B. Rostow, ed., *Is Law Dead?* (New York: Simon & Schuster, 1971); and Robert Paul Wolff, ed., *The Rule of Law* (New York: Simon & Schuster, 1971). See also the review of these volumes by Lester Mazor, "The Crisis of Liberal Legalism," *Yale Law Journal* **81** (1972): 1032.

law," unable to cope with basic issues of social justice and itself a main support of power and privilege, partakes of a deeper corruption. Worse, it is a "hidden enemy":

The "rule of law" in modern society is no less authoritarian than the rule of men in pre-modern society; it enforces the maldistribution of wealth and power as of old, but it does this in such complicated and indirect ways as to leave the observer bewildered. . . . In slavery, the feudal order, the colonial system, deception and patronization are the minor modes of control; force is the major one. In the modern world of liberal capitalism (and also, we should note, of state socialism), force is held in reserve while . . . "a multitude of moral teachers, counselors, and bewilderers separate the exploited from those in power." In this multitude, the books of law are among the most formidable bewilderers.[5]

It is easy to discount the hyperbole in these and similar statements. But the underlying mood—a disaffection from what has seemed for so long and to so many a crowning achievement of Western civilization—cannot be dismissed.

The current crisis of authority, with its accompanying dispraise of law, has its immediate source in the social turbulence of the 1960s. That decade poignantly displayed the two faces of justice. On the one hand, some courts and some sectors of the legal profession made themselves spokesmen for the disprivileged; they interpreted their mission as the enlargement of rights and the fulfillment of the latent promise of the Constitution—full citizenship for all—and the movement for social advocacy and public-interest law gained wide support. On the other hand, during the same decade the law wore jack boots and acted repressively to stamp out the fires of discontent.

As events unfolded, there was revealed a continuing tension between two approaches to law, freedom, and social control. The first, which might be called the *low-risk* view of law and

5. Howard Zinn, "The Conspiracy of Law," in Wolff, pp. 18–19.

order, emphasizes how great is the contribution of legal stability to a free society and how precarious are systems of authority and of civic obligation. This perspective sees law as a vital ingredient of social order; although other sources of control are important, they cannot be relied on to save society from arbitrary will, unreason, intimidation, or worse. Only where there is a high regard for constituted authority do people experience the security they need for genuine freedom of choice. The citizen's duty to obey law has its counterpart in the maintenance of a scrupulous official fidelity to positive law. Claims must be vindicated only through established channels, however defective these may be. Legal change is to come through the political process, not from the exercise of discretion by legal agencies responding to partisan demands. The separation of law and politics should be sharp, and defiance of the law must be put down with firmness.

An alternative view emphasizes the potential resilience and openness of institutions. It is more careless of authority, more accepting of challenge and disarray. This approach resists the equation of "law" and "order"; it is sensitive to the fact that law characteristically upholds a specific *kind* of order in the form of received moral codes, systems of status, and patterns of power. The very concept of "order" is conceived of as problematic, subject to historically changing expectations, compatible with controversy and expressive behavior. In this perspective law is valued as a resource for criticism and an instrument for change, and there is a tacit faith that a system of authority can better preserve itself, and be better, if it is open to reconstruction in the light of how those who are governed perceive their rights and reassess their moral commitments. To be responsive, the system should be open to challenge at many points, should encourage participation, and should expect new social interests to make themselves known in troublesome ways. Political disobedience should be met with toleration and with a willingness to negotiate new bases of authority. The line between law and politics is blurred, at least where advocacy and legal judgment speak to issues of controverted public policy. This is a *high-risk* view of law and order.

Each of these perspectives has characteristic weaknesses. The first, in being relatively unresponsive, may encourage evasion of the law, if only because some accommodation to different interests, values, and styles of life is required; and it may actually bring on crisis and disorder by closing off channels of appeal, participation, and change. The high-risk perspective, on the other hand, in seeking to maximize responsiveness, may invite more trouble than it bargained for, foster weakness and vacillation in the face of pressure, and yield too much to activist minorities.

While "low-risk" and "high-risk" point, in many respects, to "conservative" and "liberal," that equivalence is far from perfect. There is a liberal version of the low-risk view, one that stresses the democratic worth of separating law and politics and restraining official discretion. Liberals who see the greatest threat to the legal order in the irresponsibility of *officials* often converge with conservatives who see that threat in the irresponsibility of *citizens*. In either case, an implicit legal theory is embraced whose effect is to limit flexibility and inhibit responsiveness.

Whatever the labels, and whatever the ideological affinities, these perspectives are being tested today as legal institutions adapt to changing attitudes and expectations, to social cleavage and disaffection. The alternatives are most sharply posed when crises of "law and order" emerge, that is, when authority is eroded and its legitimacy is widely questioned; when a want of consensus undermines the validity of received morality; when means of public expression and collective action press the perceived limits of tolerable disorder; when social disunity is so great as to question the viability of a single system of justice; when alienation is so widespread as to suggest that legal authority rests on too narrow a base of participation and consent. Under these conditions of beleaguered authority, abstract alternatives become existential, character-defining choices.

If authority is in disarray, so too is the more remote sphere of legal and social theory. We do not have a jurisprudence that is capable of explicating the conflicting perspectives, to say nothing of testing assumptions or reconciling differences. "Law and order" doctrines border on the simplistic, and the radical rejection of law is equally unattractive. There is an inchoate groping for a legal and social theory that can (1) affirm the worth of law and (2) point out alternatives to coercion and repression. Some recent writings are highly pertinent, as we shall see. But there has been little systematic effort to take the contemporary crisis as a problem and work out an appropriate reconstruction of jurisprudential thought. We are hopeful that a sociological awareness will make some contribution to that outcome.

A Social Science Strategy

A major obstacle to clear thought on these issues, as on so many others, is a failure to grasp the significance of *variation*. In empirical studies, and in practical experience, it seems easy enough to recognize that aspects of the world occur in greater or lesser degree, in a variety of mixes, and with varying effects. But when we indulge in more abstract reflection this commonsense understanding fades. Logical or theoretical discriminations—say, between knowing and feeling, fact and value, conflict and consensus, sacred and profane, law and morality—are presumed capable of sorting the experienced world into determinate categories. Instead of recognizing that any theoretical polarity is a way of identifying a *continuum*, a dimension along which variation occurs, the categories are taken to be empirically as well as logically disjunctive. This is one form of the "fallacy of misplaced concreteness."[6]

A social science approach treats legal experience as variable and contextual. That canon is violated when law is characterized unidimensionally or is said to possess invariant attributes. Retreat from the principle of variation is a familiar tendency in jurisprudential debates, as when the relation of law to coercion, morality, or reason is treated as a *defining* element of legal phenomena. Univalent conceptions of law as "an ordinance of reason for the common good"[7] or "a coercive apparatus . . . for the purpose of norm enforcement"[8] or "synonymous with the power of the state"[9] may be revealing and perhaps comforting. Their effect, however, is to recreate the parable of the blind men and the elephant.

We take the view that a legal order has many dimensions and that inquiry is best served when we treat those dimensions as variables. Instead of talking about *necessary* connections between law and coercion, law and the state, law and rules, or law and moral aspiration, we should consider *to what extent and under what conditions* those connections occur. In this way jurisprudential concepts are made problematic, not only analytically (as they have always been) but empirically as well. We do not dismiss the great issues of legal theory, but we do suggest that they may yield to a social-science perspective.

6. Alfred North Whitehead, *Science and the Modern World. Lowell Lectures 1925* (New York: MacMillan, 1964, 1925), p. 75.
7. Thomas Aquinas, *Treatise on Law* (Chicago: Gateway, n.d.), p. 10.
8. Max Rheinstein, ed., *Max Weber on Law in Economy and Society* (Cambridge, Mass.: Harvard University Press, 1954), p. 13.
9. Stanley Diamond, "The Rule of Law Versus the Order of Custom," in Wolff, p. 136.

There is no need to uphold, *as a matter of definition*, a particular perspective on the "nature" of law. On the contrary, the nature of law, as of any other social phenomenon, is something to be learned in the course of inquiry. It is an outcome, not a starting point. It cannot be known apart from empirical study of interdependent and variable aspects of legal ordering, for example, the legitimation of authority, the sense of justice, the making and application of rules, legal cognition, legal development, legal competence, legal roles, legal pathology. Whatever is determinate about these aspects of law contributes to law's "nature."

Our stress on variation does not save us, of course, from the need to identify the phenomenon under study. Whatever the variability, we must postulate that legal experience has *some* distinctive attributes that set it apart from other social phenomena. The idea of law loses focus if it is identified with coercive power ("the gunman writ large"[10]) or dissolved into the broader notion of social control.[11] On the other hand, the study of variation is frustrated if law is too stringently conceived, limited by definition to its more differentiated and elaborated states.

We have elsewhere suggested a way out of this dilemma.[12] The *definition* of law should not be confused with the *theory*

10. H. L. A. Hart, *The Concept of Law* (Oxford: Clarendon Press, 1961), p. 80.

11. The tendency to dissolve the idea of law into the broader notion of social control is pervasive in the sociological and anthropological literature. See, esp., Bronislaw Malinowski, *Crime and Custom in Savage Society* (Paterson, N.J.: Littlefield, Adams, 1959), pp. 55–59; and Henri Lévy-Bruhl, *Sociologie du droit* (Paris: Presses Universitaires de France, 1961), pp. 21–22. Although most writers resist a formal definition of law as social control, the focus on "living law" and the effort to open the boundaries of the legal tend in practice to blur any distinction. Some of Lon L. Fuller's recent writings lead in a similar direction. See, e.g., his "Human Interaction and the Law," *American Journal of Jurisprudence* 14 (1969): 1.

12. Philip Selznick, with the collaboration of Philippe Nonet and Howard Vollmer, *Law, Society, and Industrial Justice* (New York: Russell Sage Foundation, 1969), pp. 4–8.

of law. Discussions of the "idea of law" or of the "concept of law" are usually efforts to explicate a range of attributes, problems, and processes. They are better understood as more or less developed theories than as ways of making first-order discriminations. While it is true that even a definition (if it is not purely nominal) must bear some analytical relation to a larger context of theory, the definition does not need to bear, and should not bear, a heavy burden of assertion. Put another way, in the study of social phenomena, including law, definitions are properly "weak" while concepts or theories are "strong":

A weak definition is inclusive; its conditions are easily met. A strong concept is more demanding in that, for example, it may identify attributes that are latent as well as manifest, or offer a model of what the phenomenon is like in a fully developed (or deteriorated) state. Accordingly, in what follows the word law is used in a way that is general enough to embrace all legal experience, however various or rudimentary. At the same time, law and legal process are understood as pointing to a larger achievement and a greater elaboration.[13]

Among recent writers, we believe H. L. A. Hart has provided the most suitable framework for a definition of law. *The minimal elements of a legal order exist when there are accepted criteria for testing and certifying the authority of social obligations.* Hart's "secondary rules" are such criteria. They are rules about rules:

while primary rules are concerned with the actions that individuals must or must not do, these secondary rules are all concerned with the primary rules themselves. They specify the ways in which the primary rules may be conclusively ascertained, introduced, eliminated, varied, and the fact of their violation conclusively determined.[14]

13. Ibid., pp. 4–5.
14. Hart, p. 92.

Without such rules, a group would risk being plagued with doubts as to what social obligations are truly binding, torn by disputes as to whether a recognized norm has or has not been breached, and barred from deliberately adapting the normative order to changing conditions. The introduction of rules of "recognition," "adjudication," and "change" marks the "step from the pre-legal into the legal world."[15]

Strictly understood, Hart's focus on rules does not do justice to the variety of forms criteria of authoritative determination may take. The "rule of recognition," for example, may only reflect a consensus that might makes right, or rely on religious or clan organization for the source of authority. For this reason we prefer a slightly more general formulation. But like Hart's, our definition takes law to be generic and protean, found in many settings, not uniquely associated with the state or with a clearly organized political community.[16] It embraces primitive law no less than archaic or modern law. On the other hand, it does *not* accept as law a mere regularity of conduct, a pattern of reciprocal personal obligations, any mode of dispute settlement, or a nexus of informal social control.

15. Ibid., p. 91.
16. The definition Fuller offers in *The Morality of Law* (New Haven, Conn.: Yale University Press, 1964)—"the enterprise of subjecting human conduct to the governance of rules" (p. 96)—shares some of those features; it recognizes that legal phenomena occur in settings other than the state or the politically organized society. But it speaks to a phase of evolution in which legal institutions strive for greater integrity. For purposes of definition, Hart's approach is more attractive because it focuses on the *minimal* elements that differentiate legal from other modes of social ordering. The legal aspirations that Fuller stresses are only latent in elementary law. An account of the conditions and dynamics of their growth is better conceived as part of a theory of legal development than as part of the initial definition of law. In our framework Fuller's "definition" points to the movement from repressive to autonomous law; but some of the phenomena that he finds built into the "enterprise" of legal ordering, such as the demand for "constancy of the law through time" (pp. 79, 80), would also characterize a regression from responsive to autonomous law.

For example, social control and the resolution of disputes are constant features of family life. Nevertheless, as long as the norms governing family relations and the distribution of authority within the household are taken for granted the family does not generate a legal order. Law emerges when questions arise as to who has the "right" to define and interpret obligations, so that the assessment of family obligations becomes subject to standards governing the manner in which authority may be exercised. A sign of emerging law is the child's ability, however limited, to claim that his parents have no "right" to impose a particular obligation, for example, because he was not consulted, or because his private domain was infringed. This approach to the definition of law accords with the way some anthropologists distinguish the legal from other aspects of "primitive" society. Like Hart, Bohannan finds law where social norms are subject to a "double institutionalization,"[17] that is, when secondary institutional arrangements are developed to assess what primary norms are to be recognized as authoritative sources of obligation. Hence, not all social control is legal: Law is selective in its recognition of social norms.

Although our definition of law is broad and inclusive, it retains a familiar analytical focus. The study of law becomes part of the study of *authority*, thus bringing to bear a wide range of empirical materials and a rich background of social analysis. The definition is adequate to the task of identifying the basic phenomenon: It locates that phenomenon within a larger framework of theory, but it does not impose unduly restrictive limitations on how the word *law* is to be used. At the same time, the theory of authority can account for the elaboration of legal experience and for the variable place, in

17. Paul Bohannan, "Law and Legal Institutions," in *International Encyclopedia of the Social Sciences* (New York: Macmillan, 1968), IX, 73. See also J. F. Glastra van Loon and E. V. W. Vercruijsse, "Towards a Sociological Interpretation of Law," *Sociologica Neerlandia* 3 (1969): 1.

that experience, of coercion, consensus, and other law-related phenomena.

From this starting point, a social science strategy can return to the classic issues of jurisprudence. These issues, however, are to be treated as pointing to, and conditioned by, variable attributes of legal ordering. In this essay we give special attention to a range of law-related variables: the role of coercion in law; the interplay of law and politics; the relation of law to the state and to the moral order; the place of rules, discretion, and purpose in legal decisions; civic participation; legitimacy; and the conditions of obedience. Each of these variables differs significantly as the context is changed.

One observation is crucial for our argument: These variables are not unrelated to one another; on the contrary, there are determinate and systematic connections among them. For example, the importance of rules is closely tied to the pattern of authority in the legal order. A regime of rules limits the discretion of lower echelons of legal officialdom, thereby concentrating authority at the top; this, in turn, sustains a close identification of law with the state, understood as a monopoly of governmental power. Of course such connections are contingent and probabilistic. To the èxtent they occur, however, the legal order comes to form a "system," with a constellation of attributes that has internal coherence. Different systems, in that sense, represent distinctive mixes of the basic law-related variables, each of which assumes a value that fits the state of the larger system.

The theory we propose is an attempt to clarify these systematic connections and to identify the characteristic configurations in which they occur. We distinguish three modalities or basic "states" of law-in-society: (1) law as the servant of repressive power, (2) law as a differentiated institution capable of taming repression and protecting its own integrity, and (3) law as a facilitator of response to social needs and aspirations. The characteristics of each type are outlined in Table 1. For example, although coercion is present in all three types, its significance varies: It is dominant in repressive law, moderated in autonomous law, and submerged in responsive law. Again, the role of purpose must be considered in each system: There is a repressive instrumentalism in which law is bent to the will of governing power; there is a withdrawal from purpose in the striving for autonomous law; and there is a renewal of instrumentalism, but for more objective public ends, in the context of responsive law. Each law-related variable must be understood in relation to others and to the larger system. Thus the place of discretion, and the legal problems it poses, are intimately dependent on the variable social contexts of official action. Discretion does not necessarily foster unrestrained authority. It is most likely to do so when power is isolated from social structure and therefore removed from the moderating effect of community involvement. Autonomous law, as it strives to control and narrow discretion, presumes the persistence of official isolation. Under conditions of diffused and integrated power, the risk of repression recedes[18] and the problem of law becomes less to restrain officials than to keep them committed to public ends. A renewed focus on purpose may then require an enlargement of discretion.

18. The underlying phenomenon is multiple loyalties. When persons in authority are also bound to the governed by ties of kinship or community, their commitments as officials are qualified by other, more enduring loyalties and responsibilities. The same phenomenon affects other legal relations as well; for example, the arm's-length reciprocity of contract is seldom observed in tightly knit communities except in relations with strangers. For case studies of the "multiplex relationships" that bind members of society to each other and their leaders to them, see Max Gluckman, *The Judicial Process Among the Barotse of Northern Rhodesia* (Glencoe, Ill.: Free Press, 1955), pp. 19–23; and *Politics, Law and Ritual in Tribal Society* (New York: Mentor Books, 1965), pp. 120, 137–145; E. E. Evans Pritchard, *The Nuer* (Oxford: Clarendon Press, 1965, 1940), pp. 155–159, 169–170; and Elizabeth Colson, "Social Control and Vengeance in Plateau Tonga Society," *Africa* **23** (1953): 199, 201, 203, 210–211.

TABLE 1. THREE TYPES OF LAW

	REPRESSIVE LAW	AUTONOMOUS LAW	RESPONSIVE LAW
ENDS OF LAW	Order	Legitimation	Competence
LEGITIMACY	Social defense and raison d'état	Procedural fairness	Substantive justice
RULES	Crude and detailed but only weakly binding on rule makers	Elaborate; held to bind rulers as well as ruled	Subordinated to principle and policy
REASONING	Ad hoc; expedient and particularistic	Strict adherence to legal authority; vulnerable to formalism and legalism	Purposive; enlargement of cognitive competence
DISCRETION	Pervasive; opportunistic	Confined by rules; narrow delegation	Expanded, but accountable to purpose
COERCION	Extensive; weakly restrained	Controlled by legal restraints	Positive search for alternatives, e.g., incentives, self-sustaining systems of obligations
MORALITY	Communal morality; legal moralism; "morality of constraint"	Institutional morality; i.e., preoccupied with the integrity of legal process	Civil morality; "morality of cooperation"
POLITICS	Law subordinated to power politics	Law "independent" of politics; separation of powers	Legal and political aspirations integrated; blending of powers
EXPECTATIONS OF OBEDIENCE	Unconditional; disobedience per se punished as defiance	Legally justified rule departures, e.g, to test validity of statutes or orders	Disobedience assessed in light of substantive harms; perceived as raising issues of legitimacy
PARTICIPATION	Submissive compliance; criticism as disloyalty	Access limited by established procedures; emergence of legal criticism	Access enlarged by integration of legal and social advocacy

Repressive, autonomous, and responsive law are abstract conceptions whose empirical referents are necessarily somewhat elusive. Much the same might be said of any social-science typology, including the classification of personalities. We recognize that no complex legal order, or sector of it, ever forms a fully coherent system; any given legal order or legal institution is likely to have a "mixed" character, incorporating aspects of all three types of law. But the elements of one type may be more or less salient, strongly institutionalized or only incipient, in the foreground of awareness or only dimly perceived. Thus although a legal order will exhibit elements of all types, its basic *posture* may nevertheless approximate one type more closely than the others. One function of the model is precisely to assess the characteristic posture of a legal order, or branch of it, insofar as that is warranted. In an older idiom such an assessment might have been called a search for the "spirit" of, say, English common law or modern administrative law. Inquiry proceeds by determining to what extent and under what conditions the attributes of one or another type occur. As we shall see, some institutions or historical settings closely approximate the theoretical model.

Our three types readily evoke, and with some fidelity, the classic paradigms of legal theory. Philosophical perspectives, such as legal positivism or legal realism, may seem in radical conflict when formulated as general theories of legal ordering. In our view they can be reconciled, and better understood, if they are read as accounting for different modalities of legal experience. Thus repressive law recalls the imagery of Thomas Hobbes, John Austin, and Karl Marx. In this model law is the command of a sovereign who possesses, in principle, unlimited discretion; law and the state are inseparable. Autonomous law is the form of governance conceived and celebrated as the "rule of law" in the jurisprudence of A. V. Dicey. The writings of contemporary legal positivists, such as Hans Kelsen and

H. L. A. Hart, as well as their natural-law critics, especially Lon L. Fuller in *The Morality of Law*, also speak to the subordination of official decisions to law, the distinctiveness of autonomous legal institutions and modes of thought, and the integrity of legal judgment. The need for a responsive legal order has been the chief theme of all who have shared the functional, pragmatic, purposive spirit of Roscoe Pound, the legal realists, and contemporary critics of the model of rules.[19]

These classic strivings for an adequate account of legal experience have always overlapped and interpenetrated. Thus Austin's insistence that law is the command of a sovereign helped fix a coercive imagery; but it was, for him, only a starting point for elaborating the formal attributes of legal thought. Although legal realism was an assault on legal formalism, its call for greater rationality took for granted, and indeed built upon, a panoply of traditions, such as an independent judiciary and a commitment to unbiased judgment, that sustained the autonomy of law. The jurisprudential debate has obscured this overlap by centering on competing conceptions of the nature of law. A social science strategy can more readily and explicitly recognize the plurality of legal experience.

A Developmental Model

A preoccupation with the varieties of legal experience, and with characteristic law-related variables, should provoke little objection. Once stated, it is a fairly evident scientific necessity. However, our second analytical strategy—the application of a developmental perspective—is more controversial and more troublesome. We want to argue that repressive, autonomous, and responsive law are not only distinct types of law but, in some sense, stages of evolution in the relation of law to the political and social order.

19. See note 3.

"Development" is one of the most vexing ideas in the social sciences. It has been subjected to sustained criticism ever since the heyday of evolutionism in the nineteenth century.[20] Yet the attempt to make sense of institutional history seems to require an appreciation of directionality, growth, and decay. In jurisprudence also there is an intuitive understanding that some fields of law are more "developed" than others, and that legal change often reveals patterns of growth or decline. Roscoe Pound is among those who have found it "convenient to think of . . . stages of legal development in systems which have come to maturity."[21] We take the view that the criticism of theories of development is properly addressed to intellectual overreaching, but that the basic perspective is fruitful and even inescapable.

Developmental models are applied, with uneven success, in virtually every field of social science, including psychology. The underlying quest is for theories that can account for unplanned and recurrent transformations whose sources and direction are built into the structure of a phenomenon, for example, the movement from sect to church,[22] the "iron law of oligarchy,"[23] the attenuation of culture,[24] the stages of

---

20. See, e.g., Karl R. Popper, *The Poverty of Historicism* (New York: Harper Torchbooks, 1964, 1957), pp. 45ff, 105 ff; and Robert A. Nisbet, *Social Change and History* (New York: Oxford University Press, 1969), p. 240ff.

21. Roscoe Pound, *Jurisprudence* (St. Paul, Minn.: West Publishing, 1959), I, 366.

22. Bryan R. Wilson, *Sects and Society* (Berkeley: University of California Press, 1961), pp. 5, 325ff; Ernst Troeltsch, *The Social Teachings of the Christian Churches* (London: George Allen & Unwin, 1956, 1911), I, 43–51, 331ff.

23. Roberto Michels, *Political Parties: A Sociological Study of the Oligarchical Tendencies of Modern Democracies* (New York: Free Press, 1949, 1911).

24. Edward Sapir, "Culture, Genuine and Spurious," *American Journal of Sociology*, 29 (1924): 401; and Robert Redfield, *The Folk Culture of Yucatan* (Chicago: University of Chicago Press, 1941).

growth to psychological maturity in Freudian theory,[25] and the transformation of the morality of constraint into a morality of cooperation in child development.[26] These theories do not necessarily deal with the transformation of whole societies or even of whole institutional systems. Whatever their scope, the main point is that a determinate disposition to change is traced such that systematic forces set in motion at one stage are said to produce characteristic outcomes at another. Thus every developmental model postulates an "inner dynamic."

The notion of an "inner dynamic" is understandably resisted by many social scientists, who fear (1) an attribution of necessity to conditional patterns or (2) a selective emphasis that reads preconceptions into history. The outcome of these fears is a disposition to focus on the historically contingent to the exclusion of systemic propensities. But consider the following comment on social and political change in fourteenth-century Wales:

The Wales of 1400 was not the tribal Wales of popular imagination. . . . a regime of large integrated individual estates had to a large extent displaced . . . the semi-communal holding of land by a group of relatives. The change from tribalism had been in part brought about by a closer association with England and with the feudalism of the Marches; most of all, however, by the growth of the state and the existence of centralized administrative institutions. This growth necessitated an administrative bureaucracy, and an official aristocracy of *ministeriales* began to develop, members of

25. There are close substantive as well as logical affinities between the model of legal development and Freudian and other theories of psychological development. A common theme is the transformation of authority in the direction of greater moderation and rationality. These affinities are briefly discussed in Chapter 2, note 2 and pp. 49–51.

26. Jean Piaget, *The Moral Judgment of the Child* (New York: Free Press, 1965, 1932).

which were often rewarded with grants of land little related to the tribal pattern.[27]

Here the erosion of communal landholding is traced ("most of all") to the urgencies of government in that time and place, especially the need to reward an emergent bureaucracy. That need, and the mode of fulfilling it by making grants of land, were more than happenstance conjunctions of events. They arose out of the character of the social system under construction. It is in this sense that we may speak, in a quite matter-of-fact way, of a built-in push toward determinate change, a source of directionality in history—without prejudice to the idea that much change is a result of "external" influences.

Of course locating a specific historical dynamic is not the same as formulating a broader theory of recurrent outcomes. But there is a close connection, because any broader theory must be anchored in just such specific patterns. Take, for example, the discussion of bureaucracy in contemporary social science. At least implicitly, and to a large extent explicitly, a developmental model is accepted. Students of modern organizations speak rather freely of three stages: prebureaucratic, bureaucratic, and postbureaucratic.[28] The characteristics of each stage are noted in Table 2. The model summarizes a large number of historical findings and places them in a coherent framework. It asserts that, under appropriate conditions, specific processes emerge that tend to transform ad hoc prebureaucratic decision making into more systematic bureaucratic decision making; the latter, in turn, is subject to

27. E. F. Jacob, *The Fifteenth Century* (Oxford: Oxford University Press, 1961), p. 38.
28. This theme is developed in Warren G. Bennis, *Changing Organizations* (New York: McGraw-Hill, 1966), pp. 3–15; and *Beyond Bureaucracy: Essays in the Development and Evolution of Human Organization* (New York: McGraw-Hill, 1973).

TABLE 2. THREE TYPES OF FORMAL ORGANIZATION

	PREBUREAUCRATIC	BUREAUCRATIC	POSTBUREAUCRATIC
PURPOSE	Particularistic; confusion of private interests and public responsibilities	Explicit, fixed, public; identified by assigned jurisdiction	Mission-oriented; flexible
AUTHORITY	Traditional, charismatic, unstructured	Hierarchically subdivided spheres of competence; communication "through channels"; formal rationality	Team and task force organization; open communication; diffusion of authority; substantive rationality
RULES	Unsystematic	Codified; blueprints for action; focus on administrative regularity	Subordinated to purpose, avoidance of rule-boundedness
DECISION MAKING	Ad hoc; subject to whims of one-man rule and to uncontrolled actions by subordinates	Systematic; routinized; limited delegation; assumption of stable social world composed of elements readily classified and made subject to rules	Participatory; problem-centered; broad delegation; assumption of shifting environment of shifting requirements and opportunities
CAREERS	Unstable, nonprofessional; offices available for sale or as part-time prizes for elites	The official as full-time professional committed to the organization; no personal constituency; appointment based on merit; emphasis on seniority and tenure	Multiple and temporary affiliations; involvement through subcontracting; experts have autonomous professional base

pressures that strain toward a more flexible postbureaucratic style.[29]

This developmental model of bureaucracy is not a historical synopsis. It does not purport to describe a particular sequence of events or to predict a specific future. Rather, it is a theory of institutional constraint and response whose intellectual function is to identify *potentials for change* in a specified range of situations. Although the model may, for some settings, roughly approximate the broad sweep of history, this is not the main point. A developmental model is a complex dispositional statement. It proposes that certain states of a system will generate forces leading to specified changes. It is helpful if it successfully identifies characteristic stresses, problems, opportunities, expectations, and emergent adaptations. These may and do suggest the direction of change, but they cannot tell us what will actually happen, since that always depends on widely varying conditions and countervailing forces.

For example, the idea of a postbureaucratic organization points to the limitations of bureaucracy as an instrument of rational action. The distinctive characteristics of bureaucracy create vested interests and other rigidities. Many contemporary organizations require greater flexibility than the bureaucratic mode allows, and they are more concerned with stimulating initiative than with regulating conduct. But no one knows how far this development can go, and it is certainly doubtful that bureaucracy can be wholly transcended. Properly understood, the delineation of a postbureaucratic stage is not an exercise in prophecy. It is a way of identifying an incipient historical pattern and a significant historical alternative.

Clearly not every "inner dynamic" reveals a developmental process. Some point simply to the transformation of one type of social organization into another, for example, the shift from

29. The close parallel between that model and our own model of legal development is discussed further on pp. 64–65 and 58–100.

communal landholding to individual estates in the example quoted earlier. But students of social change have had a special interest in patterns of transformation that result in the emergence of new unities *with larger competencies*, that is, greater capacities for problem solving. Some of that interest is practical and policy-oriented. More fundamental, however, is the responsibility for discovery. Our understanding of social change is incomplete if we do not seek out the modes of adaptation that create new and potentially viable historical alternatives, for example, the movement from status to contract,[30] from *Gemeinschaft* to *Gesellschaft*,[31] from strict law to equity.[32]

These patterns involve both disorganization and reorganization, the attenuation of the old and the emergence of the new. They are developmental, however, in that some states or stages are assumed to be "prior" to others, often in time, but more significantly in importance and function. The "advanced" or "higher" stages establish new competencies while resolving the persisting and more basic urgencies of earlier states. An obvious example is Freud's dictum, "Where id was, there ego shall be."[33] Sometimes the developmental aspect of a transformation is obscured and one must look to the context. What appears to be merely an assertion that one social form is substituted for another (e.g., contract for status) must be understood as a hypothesis that the new form contributes to a social order that (in this case) is more capable of dealing with the limitations of a kin-based social organization, for example, nepotism, or the sharp separation of aliens from members of the

30. Henry Sumner Maine, *Ancient Law* (Boston: Beacon Press, 1963, 1861), pp. 163–165.

31. Ferdinand Tönnies, *Community and Society*, trans. and ed. by C. P. Loomis (New York: Harper & Row, 1963, 1887).

32. Pound, I, 363–459.

33. Sigmund Freud, *New Introductory Lectures on Psychoanalysis* (New York: Norton, 1965, 1933), p. 80.

kin. In our model, repressive law is "prior" in the sense that it resolves the fundamental problem of establishing political order, a condition without which the legal and political system cannot move on to "higher" pursuits. Autonomous law presupposes and builds upon that achievement, just as responsive law builds upon the more limited but basic constitutional cornerstones of the "rule of law" stage.

A key function of developmental models in social inquiry is to help diagnose the capacities and weaknesses of institutions, and assess their potentials for the realization of values. The bases of such assessments are not arbitrarily posited. Indeed, the point of a developmental model is to ground the recognition of salient or emerging values in the analysis of historical stresses and opportunities. Thus to say that repressive and responsive law represent, respectively, a low and a high stage of legal development is not to argue that the latter is inherently preferable to the former. A developmental theory resists judgments based on abstract criteria of "good" law, organization, or personality. It insists that evaluation await a close assessment of actual problems, resources, and opportunities; only this context can tell us what needs are pressing and what ends can in fact be sought. Repression, we shall argue, is a "natural" response to certain states of legal and social organization, and there are conditions under which a dispassionate analyst would have to conclude it was a wiser, perhaps necessary, course of institutional evolution, if only because no practical alternative was available. In any case, it should be clear that identifying a potential, for instance, for an evolution toward greater responsiveness, does not commit one to advocating such a transformation. Although responsive law may permit a higher achievement of justice, that aspiration may in fact conflict with other worthy human ends. We need not prejudge whether it must reasonably be preferred.

We should add that a developmental model points to vulnerabilities as well as to sources of growth. Some of the energy leading to change results from inherent problems and tensions, with corollary risks of regression. Thus in personality development the child is confronted with the need to establish his own independence—a risky enterprise that may encourage him forward but may also lead to regressive dependence or withdrawal. In principle, developmental models have as much to do with decay or deterioration as with growth or advancement.

Accordingly, a theory of growth need not entail that the "advanced" stage is the "fittest" or the most "adaptive" or the most stable. Although adaptation is crucial to any pattern of development, the adaptive *outcome* may be quite precarious. Advanced technological systems, including man-made ecosystems, possess high levels of competence, but they are also uniquely vulnerable.[34] And the attainment of complex human ideals always depends on an ultimately fragile network of supporting circumstances. For this reason we recognize that in our model stage III is less stable than stage II. Stage I also has its own sources of instability, including a precarious legitimacy. Thus it can be argued that only stage II offers the promise of an enduring and stable institutional order. The developmental model can then be recast with a focus on autonomous law as pointing to the tensions in that stage that generate both a risk of regression to repressive patterns and a potential for greater responsiveness.[35]

The demand for responsive law stems from the limitations people perceive in the system of autonomous law. Yet responsive law, in reaching for a complex achievement, makes great and perhaps excessive demands for competence and resilience in the political community. Responsive law is more than an

---

34. This point is emphasized in Barry Commoner, *The Closing Circle: Nature, Man and Technology* (New York: Knopf, 1971).
35. See also the discussion on pp. 116–118.

abstract ideal, for it is rooted in historical exigencies. At the same time, we know that we speak of an outcome that lies, as Santayana said, "at the limits of what is possible, and must serve rather to measure achievements than to prophesy them."[36]

36. George Santayana, *The Life of Reason: Or, the Phases of Human Progress* (New York: Charles Scribner's Sons, 1954), p. 456.

II

Repressive Law

The idea of repressive law presumes that any given legal order may be "congealed injustice."[1] The mere existence of law does not guarantee fairness, much less substantive justice. On the contrary, every legal order has a repressive *potential* because it is always at some point bound to the status quo and, in offering a mantle of authority, makes power more effective. All this is well understood in general terms, but there has been little effort to explore systematically the distinctive characteristics of repressive law and to do so in a way that accounts for variation.

Governing power is repressive when it gives short shrift to the interests of the governed, that is, when it is disposed to disregard those interests or deny their legitimacy. As a result the position of the subject is precarious and vulnerable. To be sure, any act of government or decision at law may require the subordination of some interests to others. Not every claim can be vindicated, nor can every interest be given equal recog-

1. The phrase "congealed injustice" is from Howard Zinn, *Disobedience and Democracy: Nine Fallacies on Law and Order* (New York: Vintage Books, 1968), p. 4.

nition. But to override an interest in the course of establishing a priority is not necessarily an act of repression. An adverse and even painful decision is not repressive as long as it avoids generating a sense of jeopardy, for example, by following procedures that respect the subject's claims or by seeking ways to moderate or limit harmful effects.[2]

A repressive regime is one that puts all interests in jeopardy, and especially those not protected by an existing system of privilege and power. But every political order is repressive in some respects and to some extent. The specific interests—say, of migrant workers or homeless children—whose disregard constitutes repression will vary, of course, from one context to another. What groups are vulnerable to repression depends on the distribution of power, patterns of consciousness, and much else that is historically contingent. Furthermore, the potential for repression is increased as expectations are enlarged and new interests are asserted, for then more occasions arise when the imperatives of government may require or encourage disregard of strongly felt claims of right. On the other hand, giving short shrift to legitimate interests may not be experienced as repressive when it occurs under the pressure of a widely understood emergency, such as a wartime crisis or its equivalent. Hence, in substantive content repression, like "dehumanization," is a largely relative idea. This should not prevent us, however, from recognizing repressive law as a

2. There is obvious continuity between the idea of repression, as we conceive it, and the psychoanalytic concept of repression as a phase of the formation of personality. In Freudian theory repression is the process by which individual needs, especially aggressive impulses, are subordinated to the demands of the social order through the medium of parental authority. Illegitimate impulses are censored, become charged with guilt, and are pushed out of awareness and into the unconscious. In many ways "superego morality" is to the self what repressive law is to society: It demands uncritical obedience and is incapable of accommodating the exigencies of order to the individual's need for libidinal gratification. On "superego morality," see pp. 49–51.

phenomenon whose general features are discernible despite the variation of cultures and contexts.

Repression, thus understood, need not involve blatant oppression. It occurs also where power is benign but takes little note of, and is not effectively restrained by, affected interests. The most obvious form of repression is the unrestrained use of coercion to uphold commands, suppress deviance, or put down protest. But repression is often subtle and indirect, encouraging and exploiting passive acquiescence.

Although the legal order may employ coercion or rely on an ultimate power to coerce, that alone does not make the system repressive.[3] Coercion is restrained when it is used with discrimination, tailored to specific harms or threats; when alternative means of control are sought; and when opportunities are available for the subject to assert and protect his interests. It does not follow, of course, that coercion is innocent. Even where force is moderated, it tends to foster repression because (1) the availability of means of coercion offers a convenient alternative and reduces the need for accommodation, and (2)

3. The jurisprudential debate on the relation between law and coercion offers a striking instance of the confusion that follows from a preoccupation with defining attributes of law. Understandably, if not logically, a *definition* by which coercion is proposed to distinguish law from other components of the normative order is taken to offer an empirical theory that coercion has, inevitably, a paramount role in the legal system. A spectre of unmitigated force is evoked, and critics respond by attempting to separate law from coercion. This approach is of course vulnerable to the commonsense observation that coercive sanctions, however moderated, remain lurking in the background of the legal order. At its most benign, law may not achieve more than "voluntary cooperation in a coercive system." H. L. A. Hart, *The Concept of Law* (Oxford: Clarendon Press, 1961), p. 193. See also Malcolm Feeley, "Coercion and Compliance: A New Look at an Old Problem," *Law and Society Review* 4 (1970): 505. We take the view that coercion is better understood as an important but variable *empirical correlate* of the effort to uphold authoritative norms. Recognizing that coercion has a probable place in the legal order does not commit one to any strong conclusion regarding the character of law as a mode of governance. It only opens inquiry into critical variations in the way coercion is used in different contexts.

the use of force is dehumanizing: The subject is removed from the context of dialogue, persuasion, and respect, and the legitimacy of his claims is more readily denied. Hence, although in theory coercion may be limited to restraining or compelling specific acts, there is always a risk that it will result in the violation of personal integrity. In sum, coercive power is not repressive if the integrity of persons is upheld even as force is applied against them.

Just as coercion need not be repressive, so repression need not be directly coercive. As government achieves legitimacy, as it secures what Austin called "the general habit of obedience,"[4] coercion recedes into the background. That outcome, however, may require no more than a gross and uninformed consent. Acquiescence founded in awe and sustained by apathy leaves a wide path for legitimate but unrestrained authority. Moreover, some forms of consent are distorted by desperation, for example, when weakness and disorganization induce the oppressed to adopt the goals and perspectives of their oppressors.[5] Indeed, repression is perfected when it can forgo coercion. The key to repression, therefore, lies neither in coercion nor in consent per se. What matters is how far power takes account of and is restrained by the interests of subordinates, as revealed by the *quality* of consent and the *uses* of coercion.

In its most distinct and systematic form repressive law displays the following characteristics:

4. John Austin, *The Province of Jurisprudence Determined* (London: Weidenfeld & Nicolson, 1955, 1832), p. 151.
5. An extreme form of this pattern is discussed in Bruno Bettelheim's analysis of concentration camp inmates. See Bruno Bettelheim, "Individual and Mass Behavior in Extreme Situations," *Journal of Abnormal and Social Psychology* 38 (1943): 417. A more common and pervasive manifestation is what Marxism has called the "false consciousness" of exploited classes. A striking illustration is offered in Scott Briar, "Welfare from Below: Recipients' Views of the Public Welfare System," in Jacobus tenBroek and the Editors of the *California Law Review*, eds., *The Law of the Poor* (San Francisco: Chandler, 1966), pp. 46–61.

1. Legal institutions are directly accessible to political power; law is identified with the state and subordinated to *raison d'état*.
2. The conservation of authority is an overriding preoccupation of legal officialdom. In the "official perspective" that ensues, the benefit of the doubt goes to the system, and administrative convenience weighs heavily.
3. Specialized agencies of control, such as the police, become independent centers of power; they are isolated from moderating social contexts and capable of resisting political authority.
4. A regime of "dual law" institutionalizes class justice by consolidating and legitimating patterns of social subordination.
5. The criminal code mirrors the dominant mores; legal moralism prevails.

The following sections examine these characteristics of repressive law and discuss the social processes out of which they emerge. Our strategy throughout is to emphasize that repression is "natural." In other words, a critical assessment of repressive law must proceed from a sympathetic understanding of how it comes about. Thus, we argue, a common source of repression is the poverty of resources available to governing elites. For this reason repression is a highly probable accompaniment of the formation and maintenance of political order, and can occur unwittingly in the pursuit of benign intentions.

Repression and the Economy of Power

If we take as given the urgencies of leadership, then the most pervasive source of repression is what Merriam called the "poverty of power." He noted that "there is nothing more surprising to the holders of power, or perhaps to its subjects, than the frailty of commands in certain types of crises."[6] Authority depends on a supporting context of practice and

6. Charles E. Merriam, *Political Power* (1934), reprinted in H. D. Lasswell, C. E. Merriam, and T. V. Smith, *A Study of Power* (New York: Free Press, 1950), p. 156.

belief. In the absence of that context, however, power does not disappear. When the powerful have their backs to the wall, they characteristically turn to mechanisms of repression. They do so not necessarily out of malign intent but because they may see no other way to fulfill their responsibilities.

This pattern is most clearly evident in the formative stages of political society. Nation building is ultimately a transformation of loyalties and consciousness, but in its beginnings it is the work of emerging elites who have little to draw on beyond force and fraud. Later, as national institutions take shape, the state can move forward to provide services and win allegiance. A prior necessity is the establishment of the "king's peace," together with the "political expropriation"[7] of potential challengers. The ensuing legal order has the following characteristics:

1. The courts and legal officials are the king's ministers. They are perceived (and perceive themselves) as pliable instruments of the government in power. Legal institutions serve the state; they are not a counterfoil within it. The idea of sovereignty pervades legal imagery. This is the idiom of Austin as he discusses the subordination of custom to the supremacy of the state:

When judges transmute a custom into a legal rule, . . . the legal rule which they establish is established by the sovereign legislature. A subordinate or subject judge is merely a minister. The portion of the sovereign power which lies at his disposition is merely delegated. The rules which he makes derive their legal force from authority given by the state.[8]

2. The overriding end of law is public tranquility, "to keep the peace at all events and at any price." The "satisfaction

7. The phrase is Max Weber's, in H. H. Gerth and C. Wright Mills, eds. and transls., *From Max Weber: Essays in Sociology* (New York: Oxford University Press, 1958, 1946), pp. 82, 83.
8. Austin, p. 31.

of the social want of general security" is "the purpose of the legal order."[9]

3. Legal institutions have few resources other than the coercive power of the state. Hence, criminal law is the central concern of legal officials and the representative mode of legal authority.[10]

4. Legal rules give power the color of authority, but their use is qualified by criteria of political expediency. *Raison d'état* requires that unchecked discretion be preserved; rules remain weakly binding on the sovereign; the recognition of rights is precarious.

None of these conditions is limited to the nascent, embattled state. In fact, the most extreme manifestations of repressive law occur in the totalitarian superstate of modern times. There the idea of "order" encompasses much more than peace, but in practice the attempt to force a radical reconstruction of society generates the same primordial urgencies. Unable to count on public allegiance, the totalitarian state is haunted by fears of resistance and treason, and must constantly resort to its (now far more sophisticated) coercive resources. Criminalization is the favored mode of official control, and a spirit of martial law prevails:

In the interests of economizing forces and harmonizing and centralizing diverse acts, the proletariat ought to work out rules of repressing its class enemies, ought to create a method of struggle

9. Roscoe Pound, *An Introduction to the Philosophy of Law* (New Haven, Conn.: Yale University Press, 1954, 1922), p. 33.

10. On the centrality of criminal law in the formative stages of the state, see, e.g., James Fitzjames Stephen, *A History of the Criminal Law of England* (London, 1883), pp. 177–178, 338ff, 358; Leon Radzinowicz, *A History of English Criminal Law and its Administration from 1750* (London: Stevens & Sons, 1948), I, 4–5, 140; Edward Jenks, *Law and Politics in the Middle Ages* (London: John Murray, 1919, 1897), p. 105ff; Theodore F. T. Plucknett, *A Concise History of the Common Law* (Boston: Little, Brown, 1956, 1929), pp. 182–183; and Plucknett, *Edward I and Criminal Law* (Cambridge: Cambridge University Press, 1960), pp. 26–50.

with its enemies and to learn to dominate them. And first of all this ought to relate to criminal law, which has as its task the struggle against the breakers of the new conditions of common life in the transitional period of the dictatorship of the proletariat.[11]

Repressive domination is sharply highlighted in the archaic[12] and the totalitarian states.[13] But the problems that produce it occur, and recur, everywhere. Even in a mature and stable regime, the maintenance of public peace remains the chief obligation of government. Under conditions of widespread disorganization or unrest, the primacy of order is reasserted and overrides other commitments and sensibilities. Even a highly rational and liberal-minded administrator may have to fall back on repressive force if there is no other way of maintaining public order.

The underlying phenomenon is a poverty of political resources. In general, a repressive potential is generated when urgent tasks must be met under conditions of adequate power but scarce resources.[14] Hence, as government extends its reach,

11. Collection of Laws and Orders of the RFSR (1919), no. 66, item 590, quoted in Harold J. Berman, *Justice in the USSR* (New York: Vintage Books, 1963), p. 32. On the proliferation of "economic and official crimes" in Soviet law, see ibid., pp. 84–88, 144–151, 219–298.

12. The early polity is perhaps better called "archaic" than "primitive"; we are not speaking of the government of small, integrated communities, where political institutions are hardly differentiated from kinship, but of the beginning of the effort to incorporate such communities into larger, and specifically political, entities.

13. Thus the close identification of the state with criminal law is an attribute of both the early and the totalitarian states; criminalization, as a strategy of control, is a by-product of the totalitarian expansion of government. As Barrington Moore, writing about China, argues, "the key features of the totalitarian complex existed in the premodern world." Barrington Moore, Jr., *Social Origins of Dictatorship and Democracy: Lord and Peasant in the Making of the Modern World* (Boston: Beacon Press, 1967), p. 206.

14. A similar point is made by Hannah Arendt in "On Violence," in *Crisis of the Republic* (New York: Harcourt Brace Jovanovich, 1972), pp. 134–155.

undertaking responsibilities that strain its capacities and test the limits of knowledge, the gap between tasks and resources is increased.[15] Officials might like to optimize costs and benefits for all concerned, but often do not know how to do so, lack the means, or are pressed for time. Under these conditions the tendency is to resort to repressive measures, which may take new and subtle forms.

Thus repression occurs when limited resources invite a policy of benign neglect. Confronted with pressing issues of justice or public welfare, the government may seek to avoid commitments and resist demands. New claims are given low priority or brushed aside as illegitimate. Through neglect, the state controls the rise of expectations. It does so partly out of awareness of genuine limits to political and administrative capacity and partly out of fear that frustrated expectations will undermine the foundations of political allegiance and public peace.

While some public responsibilities are thrust upon the state, others grow out of the momentum of positive government. Repression can result from governmental overreaching as well as from the inability of the state to meet public demands. In modern penology the ideal of rehabilitation may have sprung from the initiative of well-intentioned officials and reformers. But the goals of the movement had little foundation in knowledge or experience, and far exceeded the narrow competence

---

15. Some of the repressive consequences of legal moralism (see pp. 46–51) follow from a resource gap. In lending its authority to a traditional code of conduct, the state may strengthen its legitimacy, but it also undertakes responsibility, for example, for the stability of marriage and the supervision of public morals. As long as private conduct is largely self-regulating, sustained by the continuities of kinship, locality, and religion, official support may remain mostly symbolic. But when the state is called upon to lend an active hand, as in the enforcement of restrictive divorce laws, it is likely to be intrusive and insensitive, using blunt means to regulate what is otherwise beyond its reach.

of the coercive institutions of criminal justice.[16] Instead of settling for the limited end of moderating the effects of criminal sanctions,[17] the reform spawned a variety of programs— parole, the indeterminate sentence, correctional "treatment"— that enlarged the discretion of courts and correctional agencies, extended controls over the offender, and increased his vulnerability to official arbitrariness.[18]

In other contexts, such as urban renewal, government programs have lacked the means to provide for, or even take note of, the range of individual and group interests affected. Here repression flows not so much from incompetence as from the direction of public policy to a single end. Multiple goals and interests are sloughed off as public programs take on a unidimensional cast. People become resources in the game of industrial growth; urban renewal brings dislocated communities and displaced persons; public health comes to mean public surveillance:

All the sexual contacts of a man during the last two weeks before his visit (at the public VD clinic)—and with our customers that usually means several women or men—all those named and identified by the unfortunate lover, must be reached by the investigators.

16. See, e.g., Robert Martinson, "What Works? Questions and Answers About Prison Reform," *The Public Interest* 35 (1974): 22; James Q. Wilson, *Thinking About Crime* (New York: Basic Books, 1975), pp. 43–63, 162–182, 198–209; Norval Morris, *The Future of Imprisonment* (Chicago: University of Chicago Press, 1974), pp. 1–57.

17. The reform also had other ends, including the achievement of a more rational and effective enforcement of criminal law. See American Friends Service Committee, *Struggle for Justice: A Report on Crime and Punishment in America* (New York: Hill & Wang, 1971), pp. 34–47. But insofar as it stemmed from humanitarian concerns, its chief practical significance was to moderate the punitive and dehumanizing aspects of imprisonment.

18. See, e.g., Caleb Foote, "The Sentencing Function," in *A Program for Prison Reform* (Cambridge, Mass.: The Roscoe Pound–American Trial Lawyers Foundation, 1972), p. 17; Elliot Studt, *Surveillance and Service in Parole; A Report of the Parole Action Study* (Washington, D.C.: U.S. Department of Justice, 1973).

The women are called up at their homes or jobs, visited or written to, and finally (through motivation or fright) brought into the clinic. Here, regardless of the result of the medical examination, they are classified G90 and given 4,800,000 units of penicillin— unless they claim to be allergic to it. One can imagine what family conflicts and even tragedies are created by this interference with the private lives and the bedrooms of people. Notice that those who can afford to consult a private physician escape all the official reports and investigations and are never asked for their contacts.

Thus, unexpectedly, a most progressive, liberal-minded institution, the Health Department, works at transforming our society into a police state.[19]

Whatever its origins, whether in the weakness of the early state or in the dynamic of positive government, a gap between the tasks and the resources of government diminishes the capacity of law to recognize rights and moderate the exercise of power. The needs and commitments of the state acquire a special urgency and override competing interests. The hallmark of the law becomes its association with, and subordination to, the requirements of government.

The Official Perspective

When a regime is well established, political imperatives may become less urgent and less crude, but their influence remains. Power is consolidated by jealous regard for administrative imperatives: "The system" must be maintained, administrative resources conserved, authority protected. There emerges an "official perspective"[20] whereby rulers identify their

19. Quoted by W. H. Auden, "Veni, Vici, VD," *New York Review of Books* **20** (1973): 34, from Basile Yanovsky, *The Dark Field of Venus: From a Doctor's Logbook* (New York: Harcourt Brace Jovanovich, 1973).
20. The phrase "official perspective" is from Edmond Cahn, "Law in the Consumer Perspective," *University of Pennsylvania Law Review* **112** (1963): 1, 4.

interests with those of the community. The main effect is to subordinate the interests of the citizen to the apparent needs of officialdom. That pattern has the following elements:

1. The official perspective reserves wide areas of discretion, justified by claims to sovereign prerogative or special expertise. Noting the "fetishism of the state" in Soviet law, Harold Berman observes:

Each executive–administrative organ has large discretionary powers, subject to the control of its superior organs. The jurisdiction of each is limited territorially, but to a large extent it is unlimited as regards the nature of what it may do. This means that corruption and abuse of power are controlled primarily by those higher in the chain of command and not so much, as in this country, by restrictive rules of substantive and procedural law.[21]

Closer to home, a challenge to the lack of legal safeguards in the procedures by which the California Adult Authority set prison terms and granted paroles under the state's indeterminate sentencing law was denied on the following ground:

In determining sentences, and in granting or denying paroles, the Authority engages not in judicial action, but in administrative action. . . . Under California law, after the court pronounces an indeterminate sentence, and until the Authority fixes the sentence within the indeterminate limits, the prisoner is deemed to be serving the maximum sentence for the crime in question, as fixed by statute. The legally convicted prisoner has no vested right to determination of his sentence at less than maximum, nor to parole. . . . The determination of sentence by the Authority at less than the maximum is a matter of complete discretion, not of right. This court has noted that a major purpose of the indeterminate sentencing law is "to permit individual treatment of offenders, according to the best judgment of the Authority." The Authority, we believe, is and must be free to weigh all the tangible and intangible factors

21. Berman, p. 379.

which determine whether a particular prisoner is ready to return to society before his maximum term has been served.[22]

2. The official perspective shields authority from challenge and criticism. It upholds "sovereign immunity," indulges a presumption of administrative regularity,[23] ensures the invisibility of institutional decisions and dilutes responsibility for them:

The agency is one great obscure organization with which the citizen has to deal. It is absolutely amorphous. He pokes it in one place and it comes out another. No one seems to have specific authority. There is someone called the commission, the authority, a metaphysical omniscient being . . . There is [an] idea that Mr. A. heard the case and then it goes into this great building and mills around and comes out with a commissioner's name on it but what happens in between is a mystery. That is what bothers people.[24]

3. The official perspective limits demands by invoking rigid rules and restricting access. Current concern about the overload of courts that followed such reforms as the expansion of the right to counsel reveals how deeply the judicial system has depended on its limited accessibility.[25] Traditional China had a more conscious policy of discouraging use of its tribunals:

22. *Dorado* v. *Kerr*, 454 F. 2d. 892 (9th. Cir., 1972), at 896–897. The "indeterminate sentence" law has been repealed by a recent statute that returns to courts the authority to set prison terms and attempts to regulate the exercise of judicial discretion in sentencing. See "Uniform Determinate Sentencing Act of 1976," California Statutes of 1976, chap. 1139.

23. "All reasonable presumptions must be indulged in support of the action of the officers to whom the law entrusted the proceedings." *Ross* v. *Stewart*, 227 U.S. 530, 535, 33 S.Ct. 345, 348, 57 L.Ed. 626 (1913). "The presumption of regularity supports the official acts of public officers and, in the absence of clear evidence to the contrary, courts presume that they have properly discharged their official duties." *United States* v. *Chemical Foundation*, 272 U.S. 1, 14–15, 47 S.Ct. 1, 6, 71 L.Ed. 131 (1926).

24. Quoted in Kenneth Culp Davis, *Administrative Law Text* (St. Paul, Minn.: West Publishing, 1959), p. 203.

25. See, e.g., the remarks of Chief Justice Burger in "Report on Problems of the Judiciary," in 92 S. Ct. 2923 (1971).

Lawsuits would tend to increase to a frightful amount, if people were not afraid of the tribunals, and if they felt confident of always finding in them ready and perfect justice. As man is apt to delude himself concerning his own interests, contests would then be interminable, and the half of the Empire would not suffice to settle the lawsuits of the other half. I desire, therefore, that those who have recourse to the tribunals should be treated without any pity and in such a manner that they shall be disgusted with law, and tremble to appear before a magistrate.[26]

In sum, the official perspective subordinates affected interests to the requirements of administrative convenience and necessity.

The Apparatus of Coercion

The repressive effect of organizational imperatives is also revealed in the relation of the state to its own law enforcement agencies. The "monopoly of legitimate violence" is celebrated as a major achievement of (if not synonymous with) the modern state.[27] But "the state" is an abstraction. In practice, specialized agencies are formed to maintain order and implement sovereign will. This specialization has its own dynamic. Strengthened by the dependence of government on their skills and allegiance, often removed from direct civilian control, these agencies acquire the power and the opportunity to further their own organizational interests. They can interpret the

26. Quoted in Jerome A. Cohen, "Chinese Mediation on the Eve of Modernization," *California Law Review* **54** (1966): 1201, 1215.
27. The phrase "the monopoly of legitimate violence" is used by Max Weber. See Gerth and Mills, p. 78; Max Rheinstein, ed., *Max Weber on Law in Economy and Society* (Cambridge, Mass.: Harvard University Press, 1954), p. 342. See also Rudolph von Ihering, *Law as a Means to an End* (Boston: Boston Book, 1913, 1877), pp. 230–246, esp. p. 238.

meaning of order according to their own needs and perspectives. In effect, the state shares its "monopoly" with the coercive apparatus it has created.

This sharing of power is not necessarily repressive. On the contrary, a century ago the demand for police autonomy was part of a program of liberal reform. The objective was to detach the police, not from the state but from political subordination to those in power. Police professionalism, it was hoped, would bring greater technical expertise and reduce the arbitrariness that flowed from corruption, machine politics, and the intrusion of personal criteria into law enforcement.

But professionalism can bear unexpected fruit, as when it takes the form of paramilitary organization and isolates law enforcement from moderating influences. The police become captives of a technology of surveillance; impersonal intervention, geared to coercion, replaces negotiated peace keeping and service; legal restraints are perceived as subversive obstacles in the "war against crime." Above all, claims of technical expertise undermine the legitimacy of public criticism and weaken even the most responsible efforts to achieve reform. Many contemporary critics look back nostalgically to the days when, despite corruption and in part because of it, law enforcement was in and of the local community. The "new breed" may be more honest than the older patrolmen on the beat, but they are not necessarily more capable of restraint.[28]

28. For criticism of the "new breed" see Paul Jacobs, "The Los Angeles Police: A Critique," *Atlantic* **218** (December, 1966): p. 95. The issue is discussed in Abraham S. Blumberg and Arthur Niederhoffer, "The Police in Social and Historical Perspective," in Niederhoffer and Blumberg, eds., *The Ambivalent Force: Perspective on the Police* (Waltham, Mass.: Ginn, 1970), esp. p. 11ff; James Q. Wilson, *Varieties of Police Behavior: The Management of Law and Order in Eight Communities* (New York: Atheneum, 1973), pp. 172–199, 257–299; Gene E. Carte and Elaine H. Carte, *Police Reform in the United States; the Era of August Vollmer, 1905–1932* (Berkeley: University of California Press, 1975), pp. 108–123.

Dual Law and Class Justice

The idea of "class justice" sums up the ways law legitimizes, and coercively supports, the system of social subordination. Repressive law institutionalizes class justice. Here again, it is the poverty of power that makes for repression. The weaker the resources of the political order, the more "keeping the peace" requires the state to protect the status quo. The early sovereign borrows power from the strong, thereby supporting the hierarchies of privilege. Later political institutions remain distorted by the uneven participation of the powerful and the weak.[29] The legal outcome is repressive because:

1. Law institutionalizes disprivilege, for instance, by enforcing the liabilities, but discounting the claims, of servants, debtors, and tenants. Disprivilege need not rest upon explicit disenfranchisement of subordinate classes. For example, when the liberal ideals of contract and equality swept aside the old common law of master and servant, they also diminished the law's capacity to grasp the realities of power in the employment relation. Freedom of contract affirmed equality but laid the foundations of unregulated subordination.[30] In the words of Karl Renner, with contract,

what is control of property in law, becomes in fact man's control of human beings. . . . We see that the right of ownership thus assumes a new social function. Without any change in the norm, below the threshold of collective consciousness, a de facto right is added to the personal absolute domination over a corporeal

29. Jerome E. Carlin, Jan Howard, and Sheldon L. Messinger, "Civil Justice and the Poor: Issues for Sociological Research," *Law and Society Review* 1 (1966): 9.

30. Philip Selznick, with the collaboration of Philippe Nonet and Howard Vollmer, *Law, Society, and Industrial Justice* (New York: Russell Sage Foundation, 1969), pp. 122–137.

thing. This right is not based upon a special legal provision. It is the power of control, the power to issue commands and to enforce them. . . . We see further that this regulation of power and labour remains concealed to the whole of bourgeois legal doctrine which is aware of nothing but its most formal, general, and extraneous limitations, viz. its foundation on the contract of employment.[31]

2. Law institutionalizes dependency. The dependent poor are made "wards of the state," subject to special institutions (welfare, public housing), demeaned by bureaucratic surveillance, and stigmatized by official classifications (for example, the criteria that separate the "worthy" from the undeserving poor). Thus benevolent intentions, when grudgingly supported and directed to powerless beneficiaries, create new patterns of subordination.[32]

3. Law organizes the social defense against "dangerous classes," for example, by criminalizing the condition of poverty in vagrancy laws.[33]

Repression is only one face of class justice. The other face is the consolidation of privilege. As dominant groups secure the protection of the state and exploit its authority for the vesting of rights, there emerges a dual system of law.[34] The law of the disprivileged is largely "public," operated by specialized state agencies, attuned to the demands of political and administrative expediency; its business is control; its ethos is prescriptive and heavily penal. Alongside the law of the

31. Karl Renner, *The Institutions of Private Law and Their Social Functions* (London: Routledge & Kegan Paul, 1969, 1929), pp. 106, 107, 114.

32. Jacobus tenBroek, "California's Dual System of Family Law: Its Origin, Development and Present Status," *Stanford Law Review* 16 (1964): 257, 960; and *Stanford Law Review* 17 (1965): 614.

33. See Caleb Foote, "Vagrancy-Type Law and its Administration," *University of Pennsylvania Law Review* 104 (1956): 603. More generally, see Douglas Hay, "Property, Authority, and the Criminal Law," in Hay et al., *Albion's Fatal Tree: Crime and Society in Eighteenth Century England* (New York: Pantheon Books, 1975), pp. 17–63.

34. The phrase is tenBroek's. See note 32.

disprivileged, however, we see the growth of another law, which is rights-centered, facilitative, and largely "private." The law of the privileged protects property and upholds autonomous social arrangements, for instance, for devising estates, contracting, and associating. It is relatively insulated from political intrusion, administered by independent courts, fashioned by precedent more than by legislation. Here, the state is confined to a passive role; it is an arbiter of private disputes and a keeper of rules it did not make.

Thus the dynamics by which the legal order upholds social subordination are paradoxically a chief source of evolution away from repressive law and toward legal institutions that can remove themselves from, and tame, the power of the state. They lay the foundations of a "rule of law" capable of holding government accountable. In other words, dual law builds into the very structure of repressive law a mechanism of transition to autonomous law.

Legal Moralism and Punitive Law

An enduring source of repressive law is the demand for cultural conformity. In modern as in archaic society, the sharing of a moral code lends support to social cohesion and hence is a resource for the maintenance of order.[35] This basic fact

35. Although the liberal critique of legal moralism has cast doubt on the significance of a "common conscience" for the cohesion of modern society, it is better understood as insisting that the value of liberty must take precedence over the requirements of social harmony, even if this places order at risk. See John Stuart Mill, *On Liberty* (1859), in *Utilitarianism, Liberty, and Representative Government* (London: Everyman's Library, 1910); H. L. A. Hart, *Law, Liberty, and Morality* (Stanford, Ca.: Stanford University Press, 1963); and Patrick Devlin, *The Enforcement of Morals* (London: Oxford University Press, 1959). Although Durkheim is associated with the thesis that the identification of law and communal morality is characteristic of archaic societies, he also recognized the continuing dependence of order on the "collective conscience" in modern society. In his

underlies the state's persistent concern for the "enforcement of morals."[36] An initially narrow responsibility for the peace of the realm expands to include the preservation of the mores. The criminal law assumes an additional burden: Beyond the suppression of violence and treason, it undertakes the repression of assaults against the common conscience.

Perhaps the most fertile soil for legal moralism[37] is communal morality, that is, morality cultivated to sustain a "community of observance."[38] In this context group identity is defined by common adherence to a detailed code of conduct that sharply separates members from outsiders and serves as a continuing affirmation of loyalty and solidarity. Disobedience is betrayal, an offense against the community as such, and its gravity bears little or no relation to whether or how seriously particular interests are injured.

But a communal spirit is not necessary to legal moralism. Similar patterns emerge in other contexts as well. For example, when institutions seek to establish and maintain a distinctive ethos they elaborate a model of what it means to be, say, a scholar or a naval officer. Such models provide vehicles for communicating and exemplifying the special values the institution purports to represent. In effect, the institutional code of conduct portrays an image of how the true member is dis-

---

view, while differentiation and pluralism opened the possibility of greater freedom and a more rational and universal ethics, the erosion of the moral fabric of society weakened the value of liberty itself and brought the threat of conflict and disintegration. He stressed the responsibility of the state for affirming the values necessary to hold society together. See Emile Durkheim, *Professional Ethics and Civic Morals* (Glencoe, Ill.: Free Press, 1958), pp. 42–109.

36. The phrase is from Devlin. See note 35.

37. On the idea of "legal moralism" see Hart, *Law, Liberty and Morality*, p. 6ff.

38. The phrase "community of observance" is from W. G. de Burgh, *The Legacy of the Ancient World* (London: Penguin Books, 1961, 1923), p. 95. A recent case study is Benjamin David Zablocki, *The Joyful Community* (Baltimore: Penguin, 1971), pp. 63–148.

tinguished from the ordinary layman. However detailed the image may be, it retains important elements of vagueness, for the model it seeks to convey can never be fully spelled out in prescriptive rules. Some crucial aspects of the ideal remain implicit, and the institution must retain a residual authority to invoke more general standards, for example, "conduct becoming an officer" or "being a good boy." This combination of prescription and vagueness is a general characteristic of legal moralism in the enforcement of social mores (e.g., the prohibition of obscenity) as well as of institutional etiquette.

Legal moralism is best understood as a natural pathology of institutionalization, of the effort to make values effective in guiding human conduct. By themselves, cultural ideals are easily corruptible, if only because their understanding is likely to be shallow and uneven. To give ideals meaning and authority is an educational enterprise which requires that the culture be embodied in concrete models of attitude and conduct. In the effort to establish these models, moral and aesthetic aspirations are translated into, and displaced by, detailed prescriptions upholding determinate social practices and arrangements.

Thus morality is "legalized" as the cultural ideal becomes identified with a fixed image of the social order. In that process the moral order is detached from ethics; conformity becomes an end in itself, and the critical function of ideals is attenuated or even abandoned. If the moral order were truly governed by aspirations, specific duties would be analyzed as means to larger ends, and their authority would always remain problematic, subject to rational reassessment. Moral ends would stand as judgments upon the received, prescriptive order and would tend to undermine it. Legal moralism resists that outcome and thus loses sight of the larger worth of duty in a moral order. The great cost of legal moralism is a diminished capacity to reinterpret cultural aspirations as changing social conditions widen the gap between the ideal and the prescription. That rigidity stems from a propensity to overreact to deviations from the prescriptive order. When fundamental values are identified with the performance of specific duties, the moral order is easily perceived as threatened. Because rules proliferate, the risks of breaching the code are multiplied; even trivial offenses become potential signs of weakened authority or moral decay. Any transgression can then trigger a response that would be appropriate to a basic assault on the moral premises of the community.

Hence, legal moralism makes for punitive law, that is, builds into the legal process a disposition to punish. Punitive law is indiscriminate; it gives little consideration to the particular context of an offense or to the practical worth of alternative sanctions. Its paradigmatic crime is not the breach of a specific duty but the act of disobedience per se.

The enforcement of morals is a pervasive source of arbitrariness in the administration of criminal justice.[39] These costs are most visible where moral consensus is weak and a prevailing morality clashes with the sensibilities of substantial minorities. Punitiveness is exacerbated when the moral order is beleaguered, undermined by alienation and defiance. If moral consensus is strong, legal moralism is less likely to be experienced as repressive. But it may nevertheless be repressive in another way—one that is compatible with cultural unity. A deeper, albeit more subtle, form of repression occurs when the moral order can dispense with the threat of external punishment and rest instead on inner feelings of guilt and submission. A "superego morality" emerges which, though self-preserving, subordinates the person to the demands of the social order. The

39. See, e.g., Hart, *Law, Liberty, and Morality*; Herbert L. Packer, "The Crime Tariff," *The American Scholar* 33 (1964): 551; and Jerome H. Skolnick, "Coercion to Virtue," *Southern California Law Review* 41 (1968): 588.

morality of the superego may exact heavy psychic costs: self-hatred, submissive compliance, constriction of feeling, diminished consciousness.[40] These effects may be mitigated when the culture confines itself to maintaining public decorum while reserving substantial autonomy in the more private realm of intimate experience.[41] In the Freudian model superego morality represents only an early (albeit fateful) stage of moral and psychological development. Beyond the repression of the id, Freud sees a potential, and a striving, for moderation of the superego and for the emergence of an autonomous and rational ego.[42] These and other convergent insights of developmental psychology[43] suggests that there may be psychic sup-

40. "From the point of view of instinctual control, or morality, it may be said of the id that it is totally non-moral, of the ego that it strives to be moral, and of the suger-ego that it can be super-moral and then becomes cruel as only the id can be . . . But even ordinary normal morality has a harshly restraining, cruelly prohibiting quality." Sigmund Freud, *The Ego and the Id* (New York: Norton, 1923), p. 44.

41. How culture protects individual autonomy is not well understood. One way, the depersonalization of authority, is suggested by Dorothy Lee in "Individual Autonomy and Social Structure" (1956), reprinted in *Freedom and Culture* (Englewood Cliffs, N.J.: Prentice-Hall, 1959), p. 5. See also Kurt H. Wolff, ed. and transl., *The Sociology of Georg Simmel* (Glencoe, Ill.: Free Press, 1950), p. 181ff; Jean Piaget, *The Moral Judgment of the Child* (New York: Free Press, 1965, 1932), pp. 70–74, 94–96, 401–404.

42. Note that Freud was pessimistic about this possibility. Further, he envisioned the possibility of a "successful" repression that would allow the ego to transcend the debilitating demands and conflicts of psychological needs and free the self for the pursuit of moral ideals. He saw little value or potential in "instinct" and conceived the growth of civilization as requiring ever higher levels of repression. But these views are not essential to the logic of the model, and much psychological theory has departed from them, seeing repression as a gross and primitive instrument.

43. The theories of Piaget and G. H. Mead, among others, display a striking convergence with Freud's conception of the emergence of a rational, autonomous ego. Piaget sees moral development as an evolution from the child's "morality of constraint," in which rules are experienced as rigid, external, and coercive, to a later "morality of cooperation," in which rules are rationally understood as governing the interdependent activities of autonomous individuals. See Piaget, *The Moral Judgment of the Child.* Similarly, Mead conceives moral development as the transition from a regime of "significant others," in which the child internalizes the attitudes of

port for a legal and social evolution beyond repression and toward a more restrained and more civilized form of authority. This is not to say that individual psychology can have a direct effect on legal development. The stuff of legal history is more nearly the emergence of new groups and the clash of social interests. Nevertheless, the psychodynamics of authority may provide a latent resource that can be picked up and exploited by more powerful and more proximate engines of change.

If we review the various manifestations of repressive law, two cardinal features emerge. The first is a *close integration of law and politics*, in the form of a direct subordination of legal institutions to public and private governing elites: Law is a pliable tool, readily available to consolidate power, husband authority, secure privilege, and win conformity. A primitive instrumentalism prevails. The second is *rampant official discretion*, which is at once an outcome and a chief guarantee of the law's pliability.

These two features hinder legal development in the elementary sense that they inhibit the formation of distinct legal institutions. Law remains largely undifferentiated from politics, administration, and the moral order. The "separation of spheres" is alien to repressive law.

More important from the standpoint of legal development, a pliable law has only a limited capacity to fulfill the most basic function of legal ordering—the legitimation of power. Law is always a device for certifying the legitimacy of rules, commands, or official positions.[44] However, the device varies in sophistication and effectiveness. Repressive law is a rela-

those, especially his parents, who dominate his life, to a consciousness of the "generalized other," in which a rational understanding of group activity helps the individual achieve both greater autonomy and a greater capacity for participation in society. See G. H. Mead, *Mind, Self, and Society* (Chicago: University of Chicago Press, 1939).

44. On this point, see pp. 11–13 and 55–57.

tively crude instrument of legitimation. It can give power the color of authority, but its endorsement is tainted by subservience. This weakness is not necessarily fatal, for even a crude legitimation may suffice, for example, when rulers can rely on passive acquiescence and when claims to legitimacy are seldom tested. But when consent is problematic and accountability is more vigorously demanded, a regime that indulges the manipulation of law will fail to preserve an aura of legality.

Although repressive law offers handy tools for imposing order, it is far less competent at securing stability founded in consent. Hence, this stage of development is at once primitive and precarious. Autonomous law emerges to cure that disability.

III

Autonomous Law

With the emergence of autonomous law, the legal order becomes a resource for *taming* repression. Historically, that achievement may be claimed for what is celebrated as the "Rule of Law." This phrase connotes more than the mere existence of law. It refers to a legal and political aspiration, the creation of "a government of laws and not of men." In that sense, the rule of law is born when legal institutions acquire enough *independent* authority to impose standards of restraint on the exercise of governmental power.

The rule of law is better understood as a distinctive institutional system than as an abstract ideal. The chief characteristic of this system is the formation of specialized, relatively autonomous legal institutions that claim a qualified supremacy within defined spheres of competence.[1] At the risk of contributing new

---

1. The extent of that supremacy, and its qualifications, are discussed on pp. 58–60. We shall not discuss the historical conditions out of which this institutional system develops. On this question see Max Rheinstein, ed., *Max Weber on Law in Economy and Society* (Cambridge, Mass.: Harvard University Press, 1954), esp. pp. 224–321; and Roberto M. Unger, *Law in Modern Society* (New York: Free Press, 1976), p. 58ff.

jargon, we call this system a regime of autonomous law.[2] This phrase is not meant to suggest a secure and perfected autonomy. Rather, it should convey that, at this stage, the consolidation and defense of institutional autonomy are the central preoccupation of legal officials. The phrase points to the weaknesses as well as the achievements of the rule of law. The limitations of autonomous law arise because too much energy is consumed in preserving institutional integrity at the expense of other legal ends.

The chief attributes of autonomous law may be summarized as follows:

1. Law is separated from politics. Characteristically, the system proclaims the independence of the judiciary and draws a sharp line between legislative and judicial functions.
2. The legal order espouses the "model of rules." A focus on rules helps enforce a measure of official accountability; at the same time, it limits both the creativity of legal institutions and the risk of their intrusion into the political domain.
3. "Procedure is the heart of law." Regularity and fairness, not substantive justice, are the first ends and the main competence of the legal order.
4. "Fidelity to law" is understood as strict obedience to the rules of positive law. Criticism of existing laws must be channeled through the political process.

In the following sections each of these attributes of autonomous law is discussed. We conclude by indicating how autonomous law carries the seed of further development.

2. A similar perspective is developed in Unger, *Law in Modern Society*. The theme of autonomy is central to Unger's explication of "the legal order" or "the legal system," which he contrasts with "bureaucratic law." The attributes of bureaucratic law closely parallel what we have called repressive law. Although Unger does not formulate a conception of responsive law, his treatment does recognize the inherent tensions of bureaucratic (repressive) law (p. 64) and the limitations of autonomous law.

Legitimacy and Autonomy

At the outset we should recall that the chief source of transition from repressive to autonomous law is the quest for legitimacy. Indeed, each major attribute of autonomous law can be understood as a strategy of legitimation. It may be helpful, therefore, to restate the connection between law, legitimacy, and institutional autonomy.

No regime can endure without some foundation in consent, if only because it must limit the costs of winning compliance. In the quest for support rulers invoke principles of legitimacy capable of justifying their claim to obedience. Such principles need be neither sophisticated nor explicit. They may provide only that the right to make certain public judgments is, by tacit consent, vested in a group of elders or derived from a claim to expertise or recognized as a perquisite of membership in a designated family. Principles of legitimacy—rules of recognition[3]—may be quite blunt and crude: I rule because my father ruled; I run this business because I own it. Nevertheless, even a crude legitimation invites the question, *quo warranto?* by what authority? Hence, it entails a measure of restraint on the exercise of power.

Although legitimation sets outside limits to power, those limits can readily countenance a repressive regime. A legitimate ruler may be a tyrant, whose claim to rule rests on principles that encourage uncritical acquiescence in his subjects and supine obedience in his officials. Indeed, one of the main functions of legitimation is the protection of rulers from the claims of rivals and potential critics. Thus legitimacy must be seen as highly variable in content and in effect. Different

3. H. L. A. Hart, *The Concept of Law* (Oxford: Clarendon Press, 1961), p. 92. For a discussion of "rules of recognition" see pp. 11–13.

principles differently affect the restraint of power and the opportunities for criticism of authority.

Legitimation becomes more capable of restraining power as the principles it invokes take on texture and specificity. For example, if democracy is equated with majority rule the result may be only a crude accountability. But if democracy is shorthand for an *array* of principles that speak to the self-preserving consent of the governed, then the possibilities of accountability are enhanced. Put another way, the restraining force of legitimation increases as we move from *gross* legitimation to legitimation *in depth*. Legitimacy in depth extends *quo warranto* to particular acts and policies. It is most readily attained when power can be scrutinized in the light of performance or when legitimacy rests on specifically delegated powers and responsibilities. The basic transition is from a blanket certification of the *source* of power to a sustained justification of its *use*.

Legal institutions develop when mechanisms are designed to certify the legitimacy of purportedly authoritative acts, rules, or institutions.[4] The greater the need for justifying power, the more doubtful its acceptance as authority, the more likely it is that legitimation will demand special, and indeed specialized, attention. The certification of legitimacy becomes a distinct social function, and the process begins whereby this function is nurtured and protected by specialized institutions of review, such as courts, and by specialized groups, such as priests or other men "learned in the laws." Thus legitimation breeds legal differentiation, that is, the emergence of distinctively legal institutions.

This outcome flows from an inherent requirement of legitimation. Rulers have only limited credibility as certifiers of their own legitimacy. If their claims, and claims against them, are to be judged according to objective principles, it is helpful

4. See the discussion on pp. 11–13.

if the interpreter of those principles is removed from the day-to-day work of government and if his voice is heard to speak in a distinctive idiom. In other words, he who exercises the power to legitimate has his own problems of legitimacy. If he can convince the world, and himself, that his judgments are untainted by compromising associations and that his authority derives from a peculiar competence, his problems of legitimation are eased. To assert and protect that competence, he must register a claim to institutional autonomy. Therein lies the foundation of what we have come to know as the separation of judicial from legislative and executive powers. The social process of differentiation, which brings into play new groups and vested interests, completes the job of forming the institutional system we call autonomous law.

The Separation of Law and Politics

A cardinal feature of the rule-of-law model, and a bulwark of institutional autonomy, is the disjunction of political will and legal judgment. Law is elevated "above" politics; that is, the positive law is held to embody standards that public consent, authenticated by tradition or by constitutional process, has removed from political controversy. The authority to interpret this legal heritage must therefore be kept insulated from the struggle for power and uncontaminated by political influence. In interpreting and applying the law, jurists are to be objective spokesmen for historically established principles, passive dispensers of a received, impersonal justice. They have a claim to the last word because their judgments are thought to obey an external will and not their own.[5]

5. The separation of law and politics, as a theme of nineteenth-century American law, is discussed in Morton J. Horwitz, *The Transformation of American Law: 1780–1860* (Cambridge, Mass.: Harvard University Press, 1977), pp. 255–266.

These premises help explain the acceptance of a limited supremacy of law. Political rulers can accept the autonomy of legal institutions if they are assured that the rules they may be asked to honor are founded in policies to which they themselves have subscribed (or are indifferent), and whose continuing authority is ultimately dependent on their continuing commitment. All they concede is that they will be bound by their own edicts. A corollary is that if legal institutions are to retain autonomy they must refrain from imposing their own ideas regarding the content of law. Their authority is limited by a shared understanding that it will be supreme only within a proper, nonpolitical ambit.

In effect, a historic bargain is struck: *Legal institutions purchase procedural autonomy at the price of substantive subordination.* The political community delegates to the jurists a limited authority to be exercised free of political intrusion, but the condition of that immunity is that they remove themselves from the formation of public policy. Those are the terms on which the judiciary wins its "independence."

Courts are indeed especially (though not exclusively) suited to be the recipients of such a trust. As dispute settlers, judges serve the political order by encouraging peaceful resolution of private conflicts. Whether they "mediate" or "adjudicate," their function is to depoliticize issues that might otherwise explode in private warfare or other forms of confrontation. That work is facilitated by a sustained focus on the case at hand, removed from the larger context of group conflict. The judge is not to examine basic issues of justice or public policy, nor even the larger social effects of his own decisions. On the contrary, his success depends on his ability to narrow differences and render them amenable to reasoning from shared premises. This role is so congenial to the ethos of autonomous law that dispute settlement comes to be celebrated as the most central contribution of the legal process, and the judicial office comes to be seen as the prototypical legal institution. The identification of the legal process with the judicial process helps guarantee the neutrality of legal institutions, but it also encourages a narrow conception of the role of law.

The separation of law and politics is the master strategy of legitimation. It is the way autonomous law brings legitimacy both to itself and to the political order. The strategy has two aspects. First, a foundation is laid for subordinating politics to law. In the regime of autonomous law the actions of the organized political community are not self-legitimating. The political elite may make decisions and deploy resources, but the question of whether those acts are lawful requires a separate assessment. The work of government and of political leadership has to do with solving problems, mobilizing resources, and winning consent. There is always a potential strain between action and legality. Autonomous law provides a forum for scrutinizing that strain and rendering a judgment on it. To that extent, law institutionalizes a principle of restraint in the exercise of power.

Second, in their own quest for legitimacy judges stress and celebrate their peculiarly legal, nonpolitical functions. Pressed to the point, they may admit that under their guidance the law changes and adapts. In some areas, especially procedure,[6] or branches of the law that the community has more fully assimilated,[7] they may exercise a more confident and conscious creativity. In principle, however, autonomous law insists on a sharp distinction between legislation and adjudication; its institutions are to confine themselves to applying a received law to cases in which only "facts" are properly controverted. The historic evolution of distinct *institutions*—courts and legislatures—is taken to mean that profoundly different *func-*

6. We shall return to this point later. See pp. 66–68.
7. Courts sometimes do the main job of developing an area of substantive law, such as the law of contracts.

tions are entailed. Anything that smacks of judicial legislation is repugnant to the ethos of autonomous law and a threat to its authority. It is this concern, more than any simple error in understanding the legal process, that leads to naive or even disingenuous conceptions of judicial self-effacement or mechanical jurisprudence.

For legal institutions the separation of law and politics is more than a principle of self-restraint. It is a requirement of self-protection and a pledge of fidelity to the prevailing political order. To be effective in moderating the exercise of power, autonomous law must reaffirm its commitment to the policies it receives. It tames repression, but its capacity to do so is closely dependent on a prudent self-limitation. Thus, like repressive law, autonomous law remains closely identified with the state, a *Rechtsstaat* to be sure, but one nonetheless committed to order, control, and subordination.

Legal Formalism and the Model of Rules

Autonomous law is, in principle, judge-centered and rule-bound. It is the judge who symbolizes the legal order, not the policeman or the legislator;[8] and the elaboration of legal rules gives the law of this stage its distinctive style and ethos. For our present purposes a "rule" is *a norm of determinate scope and application.*[9] This is less a matter of logic or form than

8. The judge embodies values of legal autonomy, fairness, and retribution and hence is symbolically central. He is the spokesman of law as justice rather than law as political will.

9. Hart and Sacks propose that "a rule may be defined as a legal direction which requires for its application nothing more than a determination of the happening or non-happening of physical or mental events—that is determinations of fact." Henry M. Hart and Albert M. Sacks, *The Legal Process: Basic Problems in the Making and Application of Law* (mimeographed, tentative edition, 1958), p. 155. Compare Ronald Dworkin, who defines a rule as "applicable in an all or nothing fashion," in contrast to a

of function and aspiration. No abstract norm can wholly determine a concrete decision or course of conduct. But autonomous law obscures the tension between the general and the particular, the abstract and the concrete. It strives to construe any norm as if it were, or should be, sharply precise and free of ambiguity. It does so by *taking words seriously*. Close scrutiny of meanings is a hallmark of autonomous law.

The rule-centered character of autonomous law has a very practical basis:

1. Rules are a potent resource for legitimating power. They fix with precision the scope and limit of official authority, thus offering seemingly clear tests of accountability.[10] At the same time, a rule is narrow enough to limit legal criticism and circumscribe the reach of judicial inquiry. Precise rules sharpen legal control but also focus attention on forms and details, leaving intact the substance and the larger pattern of public policy.

2. When judges are perceived as constrained by rules, the apparent range of *their* discretion is narrowed. As a result the power of the judiciary, because it seems limited, is easier to justify; the threat to political decision makers is mitigated. Accordingly, the courts are most secure when they most nearly approximate the paradigm of mechanical jurisprudence. If

---

principle, which "states a reason that argues in one direction, but does not necessitate a particular decision." "The Model of Rules," *University of Chicago Law Review* **35** (1967): 14, 16, 18. To Hughes, "rules are fairly concrete guides for decision geared to narrow categories of behavior and prescribing narrow patterns of conduct. Principles are vaguer signals which alert us to general considerations that should be kept in mind in deciding disputes under rules." "Rules, Policy and Decision-Making," reprinted in Graham Hughes, ed., *Law, Reason, and Justice; Essays in Legal Philosophy* (New York: New York University Press, 1969), p. 111.

10. That is why the model of rules is counterposed to a model of discretionary government. So does Lon Fuller, in *The Morality of Law* (New Haven, Conn.: Yale University Press, 1964), pp. 33–94, as well as Hart, "Positivism and the Separation of Law and Morals," *Harvard Law Review* **71** (1958): 593, 614–615.

judges can find a closely apposite precedent or statute, and can act out a prescribed routine, they validate their self-image as legal technicians and sustain their role as passive instruments of the legal process.

3. The proliferation of rules invites complexity and poses problems of consistency. Canons of interpretation are required. Close knowledge of rules, and of ancillary concepts and techniques, becomes a matter of professional expertise. The practitioners of autonomous law are makers and purveyors of "artificial reason":

Then the King said that he thought the law was founded upon reason, and that he and others had reason as well as the Judges: to which it was answered by me, that true it was, that God had endowed His Majesty with excellent science, and great endowments of nature; but His Majesty was not learned in the laws of his realm of England, and causes which concern the life, or inheritance, or goods or fortunes of his subjects, are not to be decided by natural reason but by the artificial reason and judgment of law, which law is an art which requires long study and experience, before that a man can attain to the cognizance of it.[11]

Artificial reason upholds the authority of received law by making it an indispensable ingredient of decision; in so doing, it displays its special ingenuity, the art of resolving contradictions, filling "gaps," and providing for needed legal change. Artificial reason is the rhetoric of legal legitimacy. It invokes what is received and authoritative, and binds itself to an expert technique of law-finding. At the same time, it vindicates the jurists' claim to autonomy.

4. An orientation to rules tends to limit the responsibility

11. Sir Edward Coke, conference between King James I and the Judges of England in 1608, 12 Coke's Reports 63, 65, 77 English Reports 1342, 1343 (King's Bench, 1608). According to Horwitz, the same idea affected the formalization of the law of contracts in the nineteenth century. Horwitz, pp. 261–264.

of the legal system. When justice is dispensed in predetermined ways, in the light of fixed obligations and remedies, the legal process can conserve its limited resources. The requirement that there be a determinate rule helps the system avoid demands it may not be able to fulfill.

5. Autonomous law, though taming repression, remains committed to the idea that law is mainly an instrument of social control. In the short run, control is easier to institute when reliance is placed on specific rules rather than more general precepts. In contrast to values, it has been said, rules are the "cutting edge" of social control.[12]

In jurisprudence this striving for precision and sharpness is reflected in the pervasive adoption of what Dworkin has called a "model of rules."[13] As a theory, that model has always been false to much legal reality. Its persistence, however, cannot be understood as a matter of intellectual error, linguistic bias,[14] or philosophical inclination,[15] or as an artifact of legal education.[16] The model of rules is preserved and defended because it articulates a central preoccupation of autonomous law. Autonomous law is rule-centered because this helps achieve and protect its institutional system. If law is governance by rules, rather than untrammeled discretion on the one hand or indefinite principle on the other, the integrity of the legal process is more easily maintained. The whole tenor of legal decision is informed by a spirit of regularity and restraint. By the same token, a "preoccupation with the

12. Judith Blake and Kingsley Davis, "Norms, Values and Sanctions," in R. E. L. Faris, ed., *Handbook of Modern Sociology* (Chicago: Rand-McNally, 1964), p. 461.

13. Ronald Dworkin, "The Model of Rules."

14. Roscoe Pound, *Law Finding Through Experience and Reason* (Athens, Ga.: University of Georgia Press, 1960), pp. 1–4.

15. For example, the model of rules may appeal to a philosophy whose cardinal value is precision of language. Hughes, p. 102.

16. Dworkin, p. 39.

penumbra"[17]—that is, with the ambiguous and open-ended elements of legal norms—is characteristic of a legal order in which institutional integrity is a lesser concern than the adaptation of law to social facts. These differences in perspective are functional. By highlighting some aspects of law rather than others, they articulate the premises of different types of legal order. They also point to the characteristic weaknesses of each type.

Legality, understood as close accountability to rules, is the promise of autonomous law; legalism is its affliction. A focus on rules tends to narrow the range of legally relevant facts, thereby detaching legal thought from social reality. The result is legalism, a disposition to rely on legal authority to the detriment of practical problem solving. The application of rules ceases to be informed by a regard for purposes, needs, and consequences. Legalism is costly, partly because of the rigidities it imposes but also because rules construed *in abstracto* are too easily satisfied by a formal observance that conceals substantive evasions of public policy.

The model of rules evokes the ethos of modern bureaucracy. Like autonomous law, bureaucracy emphasizes fidelity to rules, correct procedure, and defined jurisdictions. It may indeed be regarded, as it was by Max Weber, as the chief historical embodiment of the rule-of-law model. Weber called bureaucratic authority "rational–legal." "Bureaucratic rule," he wrote, "was not and is not the only variety of legal authority, but it is the purest."[18]

In bureaucracy a pervasive formalism attenuates the sense

17. Hart finds such a preoccupation "a source of confusion in the American legal tradition." Hart, "Positivism and the Separation of Law and Morals," p. 615.

18. H. H. Gerth and C. Wright Mills, *From Max Weber: Essays in Sociology* (New York: Oxford University Press, 1958, 1946), p. 299.

of purpose. The focus is not on results but on the regular observance of prescribed administrative routines. Although Weber stressed the rationality of bureaucratic organization, he saw a tension between formal and substantive rationality,[19] and purpose had little place in his account of bureaucratic decision making. Bureaucracy is not a dynamic institution committed to solving problems and attaining objectives. Rather, it is a relatively passive and conservative system preoccupied with the detailed implementation of received policies. Bureaucratic formalism makes sense if it is understood as a phase of the transformation of prebureaucratic institutions.[20] Like autonomous law, bureaucracy is mainly a way of overcoming the arbitrary decision making of an earlier era.

The bureaucratic style assumes that rationality is forever precarious and must be vigilantly guarded against the subversive intrusions of nepotism, corruption, and political manipulation. Therefore the stress is on barriers and dividers —to wall off the particularistic influences of kinship or personal influence, to insulate administration from politics, to sustain the integrity of officialdom. The chief bureaucratic device for ensuring official integrity is the narrowing of administrative discretion: Polices are codified; decision making is routinized; delegation is limited; authority is concentrated at the top. As in autonomous law, rules are the chief vehicles of administrative regularity. They protect institutional autonomy—the civil service—while promising those who govern a more reliable execution of policy.

19. Max Rheinstein, *Max Weber on Law in Economy and Society*, pp. 299ff, 300–321, 354–356; Gerth and Mills, pp. 220–221, 331ff. See also Reinhard Bendix, *Max Weber: An Intellectual Portrait* (New York: Doubleday, 1960), p. 410; and Talcott Parsons, ed., *The Theory of Social and Economic Organization* (New York: Free Press, 1964), pp. 214–215.

20. See Table 2, p. 22.

Procedure and Self-Restraint

The idea that "procedure is the heart of the law"[21] captures a major strand in the ethos of autonomous law. The taming of repression begins with the growth of a commitment to governance by rules; procedure, in turn, is the main visible guarantee of an even-handed application of rules. Potentially repressive authority is restrained by "due process." In the settlement of disputes among citizens and in the assessment of claims by or against the state, the legal system offers its most visible and distinctive product: procedural fairness.

The close affinity of law and procedure has its roots in what we have called the historic bargain of autonomous law. The courts undertake to defer on substantive issues of policy; in exchange, they are granted power to determine their own procedures, that is, to regulate the conditions of access to and the modes of participation in the legal process. This power is a guarantee of political immunity: With it, the judiciary can demand that whoever invokes the law's authority do so in a manner consistent with legal regularity. Even the government, in its capacity as a legal actor, is expected to move through prescribed channels.

In time, what began as an institutional necessity becomes a self-enhancing virtue. The courts claim a special expertise as guardians of due process, and the integrity of procedure becomes the legal value *par excellence*. In this expertise, and in this value, the courts find their basic source of legitimacy. Although judges are presumed to speak for established princi-

---

21. The apparent source of this familiar phrase is Sir Maurice S. Amos, "A Day in Court at Home and Abroad," *Cambridge Law Journal* **2** (1926): 340: "When rightly viewed, it is scarcely an exaggeration to say that procedure lies at the heart of the law."

ples of obligation, they must, willy-nilly, display some inventiveness in adapting such principles to concrete situations. They may claim that, given received authority, fact and logic make their conclusions inescapable. But this justification, taken by itself, is a weaker source of legitimacy than the appeal to procedure. Due process and fairness are the courts' main sources of confidence and credibility.

The outcome is that a morality of means comes to encompass the whole of legality and justice. Substantive justice is derivative, a hoped-for by-product of impeccable method. But formal justice is consistent with serving existing patterns of privilege and power. The sense of fairness is affronted when a system that prides itself on the full and impartial hearing is unable to vindicate important claims of substantive injustice. The justice of autonomous law is experienced as sham and arbitrary when it frustrates the very expectations of fairness it has encouraged. In time, the tension between procedural and substantive justice generates forces that push the legal order beyond the limits of autonomous law.

At this stage, however, legal evolution is held back by a deeply ingrained norm of self-restraint. The courts and the bureaucracy are keenly aware that their integrity can be preserved only if the "passive virtues"[22] are embraced. Procedure serves more ends than fairness alone. It is also a resource for limiting access to the courts and for ensuring that the judges' right to the "last word" is invoked with economy and caution. A panoply of rules and doctrines limit standing, defend narrow conceptions of "justiciability," preserve judicial aloofness, stress party initiative and party responsibility, enforce strict criteria of legal relevance, confine the court's authority to the case at hand, and justify deference to political will and ad-

22. Alexander M. Bickel, *The Least Dangerous Branch: The Supreme Court at the Bar of Politics* (New York: Bobbs-Merrill, 1962), chap. 4.

ministrative judgment.[23] Above all, there is an anxious concern to keep legal reasoning abstract and neutral, unaffected by substantive outcomes. A result-oriented jurisprudence, it is thought, undermines the integrity of adjudication.[24] Each of these strategies reduces the risk that courts might trench upon the political process; each makes the law remote, expensive, chancy, and opaque.

The Claim to Obedience

Finally, in identifying the parameters of autonomous law we must note the stress on authority and obedience. The rule of law expects from citizens and officials alike a strict fidelity to law. "No one, no matter how exalted his public office, or how righteous his private motive, can be judge in his own case. That is what the courts are for. . . . If one man can be allowed to determine for himself what is law, every man can. That means first chaos, then tyranny."[25] This rhetoric embodies what we have called a "low-risk" perspective on law and authority.[26] Any departure from full compliance is perceived as a threat to the legal order as a whole. Applied to the citizen, the rule of law exhibits a "law-and-order" mentality:

According to the law-and-order model, the citizen's obligation consists of unqualified compliance with the mandatory rules of the state. That those rules do or do not accord with the citizen's own

23. In the United States this deference is manifested in the presumption of administrative regularity, in the presumption of constitutionality when Acts of Congress are at issue, and in the long-upheld "political questions" doctrine. In these respects autonomous law upholds the "official perspective." See pp. 39–42.
24. At this stage no distinction is made between the two meanings of "result-oriented" discussed on p. 84.
25. Justice Frankfurter in *United States* v. *United Mine Workers*, 330 U.S. 258, 308–9, 312 (1947).
26. See pp. 5–7.

sense of justice is immaterial: he is not to judge the law but to obey it . . . This model is not necessarily more appropriate to a dictatorship than a democracy . . . However the laws are made and whatever they provide, the law-and-order model requires a citizen always to comply: thus a citizen in a democracy may be free to denounce a law and to seek changes in it through the political process, but until the law is changed it commands obedience of him . . . There is no place for his own judgments, however persuasive the grounds. To depart from the rule amounts in principle to an act of rebellion, and though such an act might at times be justified morally, it can never be justified by the legal system being rebelled against.[27]

Thus autonomous law remains suffused with a spirit of constraint. A liberating effect is evident in that repressive power is restrained, but that effect is tempered by a cautious husbanding of legal authority. Justice is still very largely perceived as the arm of social control, although the ambit of control is widened to include official conduct.

Here we see another facet of the "historic bargain" of autonomous law. Legal institutions assume authority to hold rulers accountable; in return, they are to demand of citizens strict compliance with lawful commands. The courts' own legitimacy is contingent upon their willingness to uphold the state's prerogative. Leniency is a usurpation of authority over the content of the law.

The claim to obedience finds comfort and support in the rule-centered character of autonomous law. Precise rules and definite obligations go hand in hand. For subjects and officials alike, the place of discretionary judgment is narrowed. In this respect there is a sharp difference between repressive and

27. Mortimer R. Kadish and Sanford H. Kadish, *Discretion to Disobey: A Study of Lawful Departures from Legal Rules* (Stanford, Cal.: Stanford University Press, 1973), pp. 96–97. In their argument the law-and-order model is the reciprocal of the rule-of-law model.

autonomous law. The proliferation of rules that are prescriptive in spirit, detailed in content, and stifling in effect signals the operation of a repressive regime. In this context, however, it is not contemplated that the rule makers themselves are bound by what they have promulgated. Theirs is the prerogative of changing rules at will and enforcing them selectively. Although many of these rules describe expected conduct in excruciating detail, others characteristically contain a studied vagueness.[28] The result is rampant official discretion. Autonomous law counters the disposition of repressive law to use rules as one-sided instruments of domination. Now rules are invoked to restrain as well as to affirm authority. Governance by rules means that power is closely circumscribed and the obligations of citizens are limited. And the elaboration of rules creates expectations regarding the consistency and fairness of official action.[29]

Legal Criticism and Legal Development

So far we have stressed the features of the rule-of-law model that speak to its main preoccupation—the autonomy of legal institutions. As legal agencies, doctrines, and techniques become stabilized and self-conscious, they form a differentiated institutional sphere. To guard their chief social function—legitimation—and their hard-won authority—to hold rulers accountable—the law-men adopt a self-protective, self-limiting, and conservative stance. They remove themselves from the ambit of political controversy and conflict. In this they follow

28. See pp. 47–48.
29. The transition from repressive rules to rules imposing restraints on authority in the context of industrial management is discussed in Philip Selznick, with the collaboration of Philippe Nonet and Howard Vollmer, *Law, Society, and Industrial Justice* (New York: Russell Sage Foundation, 1969), p. 82ff.

a familiar path: Religion, science, art, and scholarship have adopted similar strategies in defense of institutional integrity.

Nevertheless, within the framework of the rule of law strains, opportunities, and expectations emerge that tend to break down autonomy and reintegrate law with politics and society. The very effort to develop a legal order sets in motion forces that undermine the rule-of-law model. The transformation of that model is not a necessary historical development, for much depends on the environing context of social needs and resources. We speak here of a *potential* for legal development. That potential, however, is more than an abstract possibility; it refers to specific sources and patterns of directional energy. These are mainly modes of legal thought and legal participation that (1) create resources for legal change and (2) are themselves effective in generating new expectations and new demands.

The main competence of autonomous law is its capacity to restrain the authority of rulers and limit the obligations of citizens. An unanticipated result, however, is to encourage a posture of criticism that contributes to the erosion of the rule of law. This is not an ideological stance, for the rule-of-law model is more likely to celebrate submission to authority than criticism of it. But the practical operation of the system presses in another direction. As the institutions and procedures of autonomous law develop, criticism of authority becomes the daily occupation of law-men. This is evident in the technical spirit with which they analyze, interpret, and elaborate the meaning of rules, and in their highly self-conscious commitment to procedural regularity. This commitment puts the courts in the business of defining opportunities for the assertion of claims. Thus advocacy comes to rival adjudication as the paradigm of legal action. The outcome, however unintended, is a rights-centered jurisprudence.

Advocacy does not take law for granted. It uses the full

resources of legal analysis to argue for the application of one rule rather than another, to justify a special interpretation, to invoke defenses, to present self-serving reconstructions of fact. Thus it encourages self-assertion and a searching criticism of received authority. The long-term effect is to build into the legal order a dynamic of change, and to generate expectations that law respond flexibly to new problems and demands. A vision emerges, and the possibility is sensed, of a responsive legal order, more open to social influence and more effective in dealing with social problems. The following chapter is an effort to identify the chief features of that vision and that possibility.

IV

Responsive Law

The quest for responsive law has been a continuing pre-occupation of modern legal theory. As Jerome Frank noted, a key purpose of the legal realists was to make law "more responsive to social needs."[1] To this end, they urged a broadening of "the field of the legally relevant,"[2] so that legal reasoning could embrace knowledge of the social contexts and effects of official action. Like legal realism, sociological jurisprudence aimed at enabling legal institutions "to take more complete and intelligent account of the social facts upon which law must proceed and to which it is to be applied."[3] Pound's theory of social interests was a more explicit effort to develop a model of responsive law. In this perspective good law should

1. Jerome Frank, "Mr. Justice Holmes and Non-Euclidian Legal Thinking," *Cornell Law Quarterly* **17** (1932): 568, 586. The phrase is also used by James Willard Hurst, who speaks of the quest for "a responsive, responsible legal order," one "capable of positive response to changes in the social context." See James Willard Hurst, "Problems of Legitimacy in the Contemporary Legal Order," *Oklahoma Law Review* **24** (1971): 224, 225, 229.

2. Lon L. Fuller, "American Legal Realism," *University of Pennsylvania Law Review* **82** (1934): 429, 434.

3. Roscoe Pound, *Jurisprudence* (St. Paul, Minn.: West Publishing, 1959), I, 350.

offer something more than procedural justice. It should be competent as well as fair; it should help define the public interest and be committed to the achievement of substantive justice.

The realist and sociological tradition had one overriding theme: Open up the boundaries of legal knowledge. There was to be full appreciation of all that impinged on law and conditioned its effectiveness. From there it was but a step to a more expansive view of legal participation and the role of law. Legal institutions were to give up the insular safety of autonomous law and become more dynamic instruments of social ordering and social change. In that reconstruction activism, openness, and cognitive competence would combine as basic motifs.

What was at first glance a fairly innocuous call for knowledgeable and effective institutions carried, on further examination, a challenge of major import. The challenge has evoked strong objections. An instrumentalist jurisprudence, it is feared, ignores the precariousness of legal authority. As respect for procedural forms is weakened and rules are made problematic, officials and citizens can more readily do as they please. The effect, critics argue, is that law loses its capacity to restrain officials and command obedience. Thus students of the activist Warren Court have been alarmed by the weak justification and diminished authority of decisions made by a Court impatient with the restraints of legal artifice.[4] They

4. In jurisprudence most discussions of this problem have focused on judicial activism. See Alexander M. Bickel, *The Least Dangerous Branch* (New York: Bobbs-Merrill, 1962); *Politics and the Warren Court* (New York: Harper & Row, 1965); *The Supreme Court and the Idea of Progress* (New York: Harper & Row, 1970); Robert Bork, "The Supreme Court Needs a New Philosophy," *Fortune*, December 1968, p. 138; Philip B. Kurland, "Egalitarianism and the Warren Court," *Michigan Law Review* **68** (1970): 629; Herbert Wechsler, "Toward Neutral Principles of Constitutional Law," *Harvard Law Review* **73** (1959): 1. See also Nathan Glazer, "Towards an Imperial Judiciary?" *The Public Interest*, Fall 1975, p. 104.

complain of the "tendency toward overgeneralization, the disrespect of precedents, even those of recent vintage, the needless obscurity of opinions, the discouraging lack of candor, the disdain for the fact-finding of the lower courts, the tortured reading of statutes, and the seeming absence of neutrality and objectivity."[5] By subordinating doctrine to the achievement of desired social outcomes, the Court has appeared to further the cynicism of an "interest-voting philosophy" of adjudication, which casts doubt on "whether there is or can be any substance to the distinction between law and politics."[6] Unchecked discretion is alien to legal ordering, not only because it may free "nine old men" to enact their preferences into law but, more important, because legal institutions

---

But the same arguments can be, and have been, extended to instrumentalism and activism in the administrative process. See, e.g., the controversy between Friedrich and Finer on the foundations of administrative accountability: Carl J. Friedrich, "Public Policy and the Nature of Administrative Responsibility," in Carl J. Friedrich and Edward S. Mason, eds., *Public Policy: 1940* (Cambridge, Mass.: Harvard University Press, 1940), p. 1; and Herman Finer, "Administrative Responsibility in Democratic Government," *Public Administration Review* 1 (1941): 335. The issues as they arose in the literature on public administration are reviewed in Herbert Kaufman, "Emerging Conflicts in the Doctrines of Public Administration," *American Political Science Review* 50 (1956): 1057. See also Stewart's discussion of the "traditional model" of administrative law: Richard Stewart, "The Reformation of American Administrative Law," *Harvard Law Review* 88 (1975): 1669, 1671–1688.

5. Milton Handler, "The Supreme Court and the Anti-trust Laws: A Critic's Viewpoint," *Georgia Law Review* 1 (1967): 339, 350.

6. Bork, p. 138. Bork's critique echoes and quotes an earlier statement by Arthur Schlesinger, Jr. that indicted the legal realists for their "basic cynicism about the possibility of an objective judiciary." "The Yale Thesis, crudely put, is that any judge chooses his results and reasons backward . . . A wise judge knows that political choice is inevitable; he makes no false pretense of objectivity and consciously exercises the judicial power with an eye to social results." "The Supreme Court: 1947," *Fortune*, January 1947, pp. 73, 201. Although Bickel joins other critics of judicial activism in celebrating the "passive virtues," his argument differs in that it recognizes the political role of the Supreme Court in constitutional adjudication. His plea is for prudence, not for a sharper separation of law and politics. See Bickel, *The Least Dangerous Branch*, pp. 35–39, 96–98, 102–110, 128–133.

are made overly vulnerable to the pressures of the political environment. A too open legal order loses the ability to moderate the role of power in society; it regresses to repression.[7]

There is indeed a tension between openness and fidelity to law, and that tension poses the central problem of legal development. The dilemma is not unique to law: All institutions experience a conflict between integrity and openness. Integrity is protected when an institution is strongly committed to a distinctive mission or can be held accountable to that mission by external controls. Committed institutions, however, become wedded to their perspectives and ways of doing things; they lose sensitivity to their environment. Accountability is most readily maintained when performance can be measured by determinate standards; at the same time, the demand for accountability fosters insecurity and a search for bureaucratic havens where responsibilities are narrowly defined and easily met. In other words, accountability breeds formalism and retreatism, rendering institutions rigid, incapable of coping with new contingencies. Openness, on the other hand, presumes wide grants of discretion, so that official conduct may remain flexible, adaptive, and self-corrective. But responsibilities are more elusive when they lose precision, and there is a risk that commitments will be diluted as flexibility is sought. Hence, openness degenerates readily into opportunism, that is, unguided adaptation to events and pressures.

Repressive, autonomous, and responsive law can be understood as three responses to the dilemma of integrity and openness. The hallmark of repressive law is passive, opportunistic adaptation of legal institutions to the social and political environment. Autonomous law is a reaction against that indiscriminate openness. Its overriding preoccupation is the preservation of institutional integrity. To that end, law insulates

7. See the argument on pp. 101–103.

itself, narrows its responsibilities, and accepts a blind formalism as the price of integrity.

A third type of law strives to resolve that tension. We call it *responsive*, rather than open or adaptive, to suggest a capacity for responsible, and hence discriminate and selective, adaptation. A responsive institution retains a grasp on what is essential to its integrity while taking account of new forces in its environment. To do so, it builds upon the ways integrity and openness sustain each other even as they conflict. *It perceives social pressures as sources of knowledge and opportunities for self-correction.* To assume that posture, an institution requires the guidance of purpose. Purposes set standards for criticizing established practice, thereby opening ways to change. At the same time, taken seriously, they can control administrative discretion and thus mitigate the risk of institutional surrender. Conversely, a lack of purpose lies at the root of both rigidity and opportunism. These maladies, in fact, involve each other and coexist. A formalist, rule-bound institution is ill equipped to recognize what is really at stake in its conflicts with the environment. It is likely to adapt opportunistically because it lacks criteria for rational reconstruction of outmoded or inappropriate policies. Only when an institution is truly purposive can there be a combination of integrity and openness, rule and discretion. Hence, responsive law presumes that purpose can be made objective enough and authoritative enough to control adaptive rule making.

The quest for purpose is a risky venture for legal institutions. In the large business enterprise the heritage of the past is readily perceived as a hindrance to rationality. In principle, the organization is free to demystify its rules and alter its procedures. But some institutions, notably religious and legal, have depended heavily on ritual and precedent to sustain identity or uphold legitimacy. For them the road to responsiveness is necessarily perilous; it cannot be contemplated with easy optimism. The differences between autonomous and responsive law follow in part from contrasting assessments of that risk. Autonomous law adopts a "low-risk" perspective.[8] It is wary of what might encourage questioning of received authority. In calling for a more purposive and open legal order, the advocates of responsive law opt for a "high-risk" alternative.

The following sections examine the main characteristics of responsive law, pointing to the problems as well as to the aspirations of that stage. In our view strong forces press modern law to develop in that direction, but the emergent outcome is precarious and unstable. In outline, the argument is as follows:

1. The dynamics of legal development increase the authority of purpose in legal reasoning.
2. Purpose makes legal obligation more problematic, thereby relaxing law's claim to obedience and opening the possibility of a less rigid and more civil conception of public order.
3. As law gains openness and flexibility, legal advocacy takes on a political dimension, generating forces that help correct and change legal institutions but threaten to undermine institutional integrity.
4. Finally, we turn to the most difficult problem of responsive law: In an environment of pressure the continuing authority of legal purpose and the integrity of the legal order depend on the design of more competent legal institutions.

The Sovereignty of Purpose

In the transition from autonomy to responsiveness the critical step is the *generalization* of law's objectives. Particular

8. See pp. 5–7.

rules, policies, and procedures come to be regarded as instrumental and expendable. They may be respected as funded experience, but they cease to define the commitments of the legal order. Instead, the emphasis shifts to more general ends that contain the premises of policy and tell "the business we are really in." Thus a distinctive feature of responsive law is the search for *implicit values* in rules and policies. A familiar example is the law of due process. As a constitutional doctrine "due process" may be regarded as just a name for an array of rules, historically defined, safeguarding rights of notice, hearing, jury trial, and the like. This notion of "fixed" due process contrasts with a more "flexible" interpretation that sees rules as bound to specific problems and contexts, and undertakes to identify the values at stake in procedural protection.[9] As these values are articulated, they offer authoritative criteria for criticizing existing rules, generating new rules, and guiding the extension of due process to new institutional settings.[10]

Similarly, the generalization of purpose is a key source of flexibility in the modern organization. A university, for example, takes a step toward responsiveness when it learns to distinguish what is truly necessary for the pursuit of higher learning from what it has come to take for granted in its

9. On "fixed" and "flexible" interpretations of due process see Sanford H. Kadish, "Methodology and Criteria in Due Process Adjudication—A Survey and Criticism," *Yale Law Journal* **66** (1957): 319. For efforts to elaborate "flexible" due process see Martin P. Golding, "Preliminaries to the Study of Procedural Justice," in Graham Hughes, ed., *Law, Reason and Justice* (New York: New York University Press, 1969), p. 71; Robert S. Summers, "Evaluating and Improving Legal Process—A Plea for 'Process Values,'" *Cornell Law Review* **60** (1974): 1; Kenneth I. Winston, "Self-Incrimination in Context: Establishing Procedural Protections in Juvenile and College Disciplinary Proceedings," *Southern California Law Review* **48** (1975): 813.

10. An example of this reasoning is the extension of due process to "private government." See Philip Selznick, with the collaboration of Philippe Nonet and Howard Vollmer, *Law, Society and Industrial Justice* (New York: Russell Sage Foundation, 1969), pp. 164–178, 250ff.

traditions and routines. Conversely, bureaucracy is criticized for its propensity to transform means—rules and operational objectives of all kinds—into ends.

The concern for purpose in law has its roots in the development of autonomous law. Even in a rule-centered legal order, reasoning must frequently appeal from rule to purpose, to reduce the arbitrariness of literal interpretation or to restrain officials from acting *ultra vires*, that is, beyond the limits of delegated authority. The more sophisticated autonomous law becomes, the more it must look to purpose in the elaboration of rules. Responsive law builds on that experience. Indeed, there is no radical break because artificial reason contains the seed of its own mitigation.

Taking rules seriously is a casuistic art and an ambiguous lawyerly virtue. It is an art that points to the limits of authority as well as to its reach. If rules are to be applied with precision, the classification of events must be accurate. When problems occur and ambiguities are revealed, judges must evolve authoritative ways of resolving them. These and other demands generate a diversity of legal materials. Even though the focus remains on rules, we see the elaboration of concepts, doctrines, maxims, and principles. All of these materials provide guidelines for the elaboration and application of rules. At the same time, they introduce openness and flexibility into legal judgment.

Most important, for our argument, is the interplay of rule and principle. For here a source of change is built into the legal order. Rules necessarily depend for their relevance and viability on appropriate historical conditions. As circumstances alter, rules must be refashioned, not only to meet the needs of policy but also to protect the authority of the rules themselves and the integrity of their application. In this process, guidance is drawn from authoritative principles such as concepts of fairness or democracy, or the idea that no one should profit from his own wrong, thus upholding the continuity of law while facilitating legal change. When Fuller underscores the centrality of purpose in the legal enterprise[11] or when Dworkin and Hughes look to principle and policy as foundations of legal reasoning,[12] they express the modern aspiration for a legal order that is effective in dealing with change.

11. Lon L. Fuller, "Positivism and Fidelity to Law—A Reply to Professor Hart," *Harvard Law Review* **71** (1958): 630, 667. See also Fuller, "Human Purpose and Natural Law," *Journal of Philosophy* **53** (1956): 697.

12. Dworkin, "The Model of Rules"; Hughes, "Rules, Policy and Decision-making." Also, Torstein Eckhoff, "Guiding Standards in Legal Reasoning," *Current Legal Problems* **29** (1976): 205. In his more recent writings, esp. "Hard Cases," *Harvard Law Review* **88** (1975): 1057, Dworkin appears to have retreated from his earlier views on this matter. In "The Model of Rules" he had argued that "principles, policies, and other standards," (p. 22) all of which differ from rules by their higher generality, provide authoritative grounds for legal argument and decision even though they may not be traceable to explicit legislative enactment. A theory of *law* that ignored their authority would therefore not be true "to the complexity and sophistication" of legal institutions. In "Hard Cases" Dworkin's focus shifts to a much narrower concern, the theory of *adjudication*. Furthermore, he proposes a sharp distinction between "principle" and "policy," and argues that "judicial decisions . . . characteristically are and should be generated by principle not policy" (p. 1060). The key to that distinction, he claims, is that "principles are propositions that describe rights" whereas "policies are propositions that describe goals" (p. 1067). In our view the "rights thesis," as Dworkin calls his new approach, presents an excessively narrow picture of the role of purpose or values in legal argument. Its narrowness stems in part from a limited focus on judicial decisions. Granted the need for a theory of the distinctive attributes of adjudication, such a theory cannot do justice to the many diverse manifestations of legal reasoning, for example, the way an administrative agency interprets its mandate. We discuss this point further on pp. 106–110. More important, Dworkin's account of the distinction between principle and policy makes no room for a large and important class of legal standards that do not "describe rights" but whose authority, like that of principle, does not depend on explicit legislative decision. They are *institutionalized* policies such as the policy of leaving education to local government or received conceptions of the role of collective bargaining in labor law or official doctrines defining, say, the responsibilities of the Corps of Engineers. The authority of these policies derives from a *history* of more limited decisions that warrants inferring a larger, enduring commitment that goes beyond a series of discrete legislative compromises. Such standards do have a place in judicial as well as administrative decisions, and so they should. It is possible of course that Dworkin means "rights" in such a broad sense that all institutionalized

When law stresses principle and purpose a rich resource is available for criticizing the authority of specific rules. Purpose sustains the quest for what we earlier called "legitimacy in depth."[13] Although a rule may bear the stamp of official authority—that is, meet the "pedigree test" of legal validity[14]—it is held open to reassessment in the light of its consequences for the values at stake. Autonomous law recoils from the unsettling effect of purposive thinking. It prefers rules whose authority is definite and certain, and thus assumes that the world law governs is a stable world whose features are readily classified. The "model of rules" is upheld precisely because it directs the courts, as they interpret a rule, to seek a "core" of settled meaning and to reduce the "penumbra" of ambiguity.[15]

There is much warrant for such caution and restraint. As purpose weakens the authority of rules, it widens the place of discretion in legal judgment. How far the authority of purpose can replace the authority of rules is open to serious question. It is relatively easy to accept the *critical* authority of purpose in the interpretation and evaluation of specific rules, policies, or operational goals. It is more difficult to have confidence in the *affirmative* authority of purpose, that is, in purpose as a guide for directing the course of policy development.

The fundamental contribution of purpose is the enhancement of rationality in legal reasoning. One should not be surprised, therefore, that with the growth of purposiveness in

---

policies would qualify as "principles," or that he means "policies" in such a narrow sense that no institutionalized standard could count as a policy. If so, in either case, the definitional gambit would render his argument a tautology. One would also have to conclude that such a simple dichotomy does violence "to the complexity and sophistication" of legal ideas.

13. See p. 56.

14. The phrase "pedigree test" is Dworkin's in "The Model of Rules," p. 17.

15. H. L. A. Hart, "Positivism and the Separation of Law and Morals," *Harvard Law Review* **71** (1958): esp. p. 607ff. See also the discussion on pp. 60–65.

law it becomes ever more difficult to distinguish legal analysis from policy analysis, legal rationality from other forms of systematic decision making. A sign of the change is the waning of "artificial reason." Legal sophistication fosters a gradual elimination of arcane language, fictional classification, and tortured analogies. Freed from formalism and ritual, legal inquiry can be more systematic and more empirical. This evolution offers the promise of a more effective law. But the process of demystification is more immediate and more threatening. Legal judgment loses its oracular force, and the jurists are robbed of their most visible claim to special expertise.[16]

Purposive legal thought counteracts the tendency of officials to retreat behind rules and evade responsibility.[17] We noted earlier how autonomous law, like modern bureaucracy, encourages a restrictive view of official obligation. Concerned mainly with the restraint of authority, it induces legal institutions to construe their powers narrowly, shy away from policy issues, hide behind a veil of neutrality, and avoid initiative. When accountability is to more general ends, dedication to rules is no longer enough to shield officials from criticism. But to generalize responsibilities is to run the risk of diluting them. General ends tend to be impotent, that is, so abstract and vague that they offer neither guidance in decision nor clear standards of evaluation.

For purpose to gain affirmative as well as critical authority, law must be able to *elaborate*, as it generalizes, the mandates of legal institutions. Hence, a critical phase of responsive law is the definition of mission, that is, the translation of general purpose into specific objectives.

To some extent purposiveness facilitates the elaboration of

16. This point is also discussed in Philip Selznick, "The Ethos of American Law," in Irving Kristol and Paul Weaver, eds., *The Americans: 1976* (Lexington, Mass.: Lexington Books, 1976), p. 218.

17. See pp. 62–68.

legal mandates, because it calls for inquiry into (1) substantive
outcomes and (2) what is factually needed for effective dis-
charge of institutional responsibilities. In other words, purposive law is *result-oriented*, thus departing sharply from the
classic image of justice blind to consequence. It does not follow
that purposive law is less committed to even-handed application of legal standards in individual cases. The concern is with
legislative rather than adjudicative facts, with factual *patterns*
and with the *systematic* effects of alternative policies, rather
than with particular outcomes.

So broad an inquiry, however, may do more to frustrate than
facilitate the development of policy. It is more immediately
helpful when it is limited to the testing of means in the light
of fixed, predetermined ends. As a wider range of consequences
is studied, including the sacrifice of other values, inquiry tends
to undermine the "self-conscious attempt to use law as a means
toward the attainment of some end."[18] The more wide-ranging

18. William E. Nelson, "The Impact of the Anti-Slavery Movement upon
Styles of Judicial Reasoning in Nineteenth Century America," *Harvard
Law Review* **87** (1974): 513, 515. Agreeing with Horwitz [Morton J.
Horwitz, *The Transformation of American Law 1780–1860* (Cambridge,
Mass.: Harvard University Press, 1977), chap. 1] and earlier observers
such as Llewellyn [Karl N. Llewellyn, *The Common Law Tradition* (Boston:
Little, Brown, 1960), pp. 36–37, 62–75, 421–426], Nelson argues that an
"instrumentalist" conception of law came to govern judicial reasoning under
the American common law of the first half of the nineteenth century. The
evidence suggests that in matters of property, contract, and torts the courts
of that time felt able to bend or discard the narrow rules of earlier precedents that were found incongruent with a commonsense understanding of
proper business conduct. In addition, emerging doctrines included some
very general appeals to the requirements of commercial and industrial
growth, a fact that prompts Horwitz to characterize them as "utilitarian" as
well as instrumental (Horwitz, p. 33.). Of course neither Nelson nor
Horwitz argues that courts then made law by applying a utilitarian calculus;
the judges were just thinking like "practical men" (Horwitz, p. 34). Perhaps it can only be said that references to vaguely utilitarian notions added
to their decisions some rhetoric that was symbolically appropriate to the
times. A long series of such small practical adaptations over a long period

legal inquiry becomes, the more it encourages a more sophisticated pragmatism, in the spirit of John Dewey, which regards ends as problematic and subject to reconstruction in the light of their costs. In that perspective values are always multiple, interdependent, and potentially conflicting.[19] Therefore a pragmatic approach runs the risk of aggravating the elusiveness of purpose and of degenerating into an ad hoc, unguided "balancing" of competing goals and interests.[20]

Insofar as the legal mind retains from the heritage of autonomous law a special skill in testing the continuity of new

resulted in transforming a private law suited to the practical needs of a stable agrarian economy into one more suited to the practical needs of an expanding commercial and industrial economy. In that process the courts and the law were only passively adaptive. Their readiness to embrace the common sense of practical men is of course a significant departure from the legal formalism of other eras. But it falls far short of the kind of "instrumentalism" that suggests a deliberate effort to use law as a resource in the pursuit of some defined public purpose or value.

19. Compare this argument with Trubek's distinction between "statist" and "pluralist" types of legal instrumentalism: David Trubek, "Toward a Social Theory of Law: An Essay on the Study of Law and Development," *Yale Law Journal* **82** (1972): 1, 4–6; 18–21; 37–39. The former subordinates all values and interests to the pursuit of a single overriding priority determined by "the state" and hence tends to be repressive in our sense. The latter is informed by a wider array of participants and is therefore able to take account of multiple values and interests. In our view instrumentalism becomes responsive insofar as the inquiry that informs the calculation of means is more open and inclusive, so that the quest for greater effectiveness is moderated by a greater consciousness of costs. As we point out, responsive instrumentalism is risky insofar as it makes purpose vulnerable to attenuation.

20. The drift from pragmatism to unguided "balancing" is illustrated by the "incrementalist" account of decision making in administration. See, esp., Charles Lindblom, "The Science of Muddling-Through," *Public Administration Review* **19** (1959): 79; David Braybrooke and Charles Lindblom, *A Strategy of Decision: Policy Evaluation as a Social Process* (New York: Free Press, 1963); and Charles Lindblom, *The Intelligence of Democracy* (New York: Free Press, 1965). For a critical review of the incrementalist doctrine, see Philippe Nonet, "Taking Purpose Seriously," in Gray Dorsey, ed., *Equality and Freedom: International and Comparative Jurisprudence* (Dobbs Ferry, N.Y.: Oceana Publications, 1977), III, pp. 905–923.

decisions with received authority, it may help resist ad hoc judgment. It can do so by pressing for objective and generalizable criteria,[21] reconstructing and probing the implicit premises of decision, rigorously stating policy alternatives, and reformulating the principles that support received authority. But ultimately the continuing affirmation of purpose requires energies and resources that cannot be called forth by legal invention alone. A point is soon reached where only larger resources will permit preserving the integrity of ends (say, upholding a policy of limited growth) while taking effective account of their costs (making up for the loss of business and jobs). At that point a poverty of resources would force either retreat from purpose or regression to a more single-minded and repressive instrumentalism, one capable of ignoring, say, that the order to close a polluting factory will cause unemployment.[22]

Therefore in concluding this section we should note that although the techniques and perspectives of legal reason can do much to enhance the *critical* authority of purpose, their contribution to *affirmative* authority is more modest and inescapably contingent on the resources society is willing to commit to the realization of legal ends. Thus the affirmation of purpose requires a union of legal authority and political will.

---

21. For example, the doctrine of "substantial performance" moderates the effects that would follow from strict, literal interpretations of the terms of a contract, but it offers a general standard whose requirements in any particular case can be specified by a factual assessment of the context. The quest for such formulations is a mark of legislative draftsmanship. It is a manifestation of the striving for what Dworkin calls "articulate consistency," which "condemns the practice of making decisions that seem right in isolation, but cannot be brought within some comprehensive theory of general principles and policies that is consistent with other decisions also thought right." Ronald Dworkin, "Hard Cases," *Harvard Law Review* **88** (1975): 1057, 1064.

22. For an example of this problem see Irving Kristol, "The Environmental Crusade," *The Wall Street Journal* (December 16, 1974).

Obligation and Civility

If principle and purpose are resources for the criticism of rules, a cost (or benefit) is the erosion of authority. An attenuation of the citizen's obligation to obey follows hard upon the quest for more flexible rule making. As the environing context of legal precepts is enriched, the validity of a rule is more readily brought into question. As the variety of authoritative materials is enlarged, more defenses are available against claims to obedience, and more opportunities arise for the exercise of autonomous judgment.

Like the ascendance of purpose, the weakening of obligations has its source in the complexity and sophistication that accompany the development of autonomous law. It is the offspring of what may be called the *paradox of precision.* Doctrines are elaborated because judges, litigants, and other participants in the legal process need resources for interpreting and specifying the meaning of rules. At the same time, however, they offer grounds for questioning what the law commands. Born in the service of legal certainty, precision becomes a handmaiden of sensitive judgment.

Among the most striking features of a developed legal system is the extraordinary *variability* of legal authority. There grow, in Bickel's words, "numerous laws and regulations of vastly differing orders of importance. The process is . . . too complex, diverse and resourceful to subsume an unvarying duty to obey all laws."[23] All legal materials are authoritative, but some are more authoritative than others.[24] Differential

23. Alexander M. Bickel, *The Morality of Consent* (New Haven, Conn.: Yale University Press, 1975), pp. 65–66.

24. This variation is often obscured because the *authority* of a legal rule or decision is confused with its *finality.* A legislature or tribunal may have the last word on the issue it decides, but its decisions are not all equally important or equally persuasive.

authority depends on many factors, including the explicitness and clarity of rules and opinions, consistency of enforcement, attenuation of consent. The relatively weak authority of a statute is manifested, for example, in restrictive interpretations by the courts, in reluctance to prosecute or punish infractions, or in special efforts to revitalize a rule. A judicial opinion may be eroded over time, "sapped of vitality,"[25] even as it retains some measure of authority. "Decisions of this court," wrote Justice Frankfurter, "do not have equal intrinsic authority."[26]

Furthermore, rules differ markedly in how and to what extent they impose obligations. These variations reflect their different contributions to legal ordering. Some legal norms, such as liability for negligence, only set a standard, and leave much room for autonomous judgment in deciding how to comply. Even specific prescriptions vary in their claim to obedience. A prohibition whose infraction is "punished" by a nominal fine may be taken as only imposing a kind of tax on an otherwise legitimate activity. Some rules—for example, rules for forming a contract or a corporation, making a will, or applying for a license—are facilitative, not prescriptive. Their main sanction is failure to achieve one's purpose. The issue of duty may hardly arise, at least initially.

Finally, and most important, legal casuistry generates elaborate techniques for weighing the *situational* authority of legal precepts. The abstract or dogmatic authority of a rule, which is a function of its formal validity and its substantive merit as a general policy, never fully determines what force the rule may have under the circumstances of a particular case. In a concrete situation a rule may clash with other precepts, which

25. Charles A. Wright, "The Constitution on Campus," *Vanderbilt Law Review* **22** (1969): 1027, 1040. Wright says of "one of the less admired efforts of Justice Holmes" that "time has long since sapped the decision of any vitality." The decision referred to is *Commonwealth* v. *Davis*, 162 Mass. 510, 39 N. E. 113 (1895), *affirmed*, 167 U.S. 43 (1897).

26. *Adamson* v. *Calif.*, 332 U.S. 46, 56 (1947).

may then qualify its claim to obedience, as when a rule against trespass is weighed against the right of free speech. A balancing of values takes place, which in theory at least is strongly influenced by an assessment of the facts.

These considerations suggest that in a developed system the logic of legal judgment becomes closely congruent with the logic of moral and practical judgment.[27] As the law becomes more open-textured, as its sources are enriched, as its cognitive competence is raised, legal casuistry loses its distinctiveness.[28] To determine the legal rights and wrongs of a particular case is to take account of multiple ends, situational constraints, and practical alternatives. Much the same may be said of the process of fixing moral obligations or of prudent, practical decision making.

A significant manifestation of this evolution is a weakening of criminal law. The bluntness of penal sanctions makes criminal justice inherently crude and alien to the spirit of a purposive legal order. Criminal punishment is seldom an effective way of correcting harms. At the same time, it is potentially severe and therefore is hemmed in by procedural formalism.[29] To restrain the use of criminal sanctions, the principle of legality (in the traditional sense of *nullum crimen sine lege*[30]) requires a narrow definition of the *act* that warrants punish-

27. This point is elaborated in Mortimer R. Kadish and Sanford H. Kadish, *Discretion to Disobey: A Study of Lawful Departures from Legal Rules* (Stanford Ca.: Stanford University Press, 1973), pp. 211–216.

28. On the other ways law loses its distinctiveness at this stage, see pp. 82–83, 96–97, 110–113, 117–118.

29. For these reasons the criminal sanction is especially ill suited as an instrument of regulation. See, e.g., Alfred Blumrosen, "Administrative Creativity: The First Year of the Equal Employment Opportunity Commission," *The George Washington Law Review* 38 (1970): 695, 729, 731.

30. "No crime without a law." Strictly understood, this principle means that criminal prohibitions may be enacted only by statutes (*lex*), not by courts exercising judicial discretion. In this sense, it has not been fully accepted in the common law tradition. In its broader sense, the principle requires that the rules of criminal law be narrowly construed, even when their formal sources are judicial precedents.

ment. But as legal judgment becomes more discriminating, it is pressed to look beyond acts to contexts, with all that implies for the erosion of rules, the multiplication of excuses, the growth of complex doctrines of responsibility—and the corollary risk of excessive reliance on psychiatric and social-scientific "expertise." These risks are inherent in the quest for greater precision, including more subtle and more rigorous ways of analyzing the overlapping categories of crime, tort, deviance, and incompetence.

In recognizing the complexity of legal judgment and relaxing the claim to obedience, responsive law points to a larger ideal. It brings a promise of *civility* to the way law is used to define and maintain public order. In the contemporary idiom the idea of civility tends to be reduced to good manners or, at most, decorum in public places. In a more general and more classical sense, civility is an attribute of political life. Civil politics is politics that affirms the central value of citizenship—the principle that no member of a genuine polity may remain unprotected. Its special concern is the maintenance of a moral community—what Edward Shils calls a "sense of substantial affinity"[31]—in a political context where individuality, diversity, and hence conflict are presumed and accepted. Therefore respect is the salient virtue: All who share a social space are granted a presumption of legitimacy. There is a commitment to widen the sense of belonging and to avoid attitudes and postures that read people out of the community. Standards of civility extend to the exercise of authority as well as to civic participation. At both levels civility calls for a spirit of moderation and openness.

Purposive law contributes to civility because it is informed

31. Edward Shils, *The Intellectuals and the Powers and Other Essays* (Chicago: University of Chicago Press, 1972), p. 61. On civility see also Howard S. Becker and Irving Louis Horowitz, "The Culture of Civility," in Howard S. Becker, ed., *Culture and Civility in San Francisco* (New Brunswick, N.J.: Transaction Books, 1971), pp. 4–19.

by an "ethic of responsibility" rather than an "ethic of ultimate ends."[32] In the latter "the believer . . . feels 'responsible' only for seeing to it that the flame of pure intentions is not quenched."[33] But in the ethic of responsibility "one has to give an account of the foreseeable results of one's actions,"[34] and hence to consider multiple interests and competing values. Thus ideology is a persistent threat to civility, for it undermines purposive and responsible thinking. Ideologues refuse to recognize the limited and partial nature of their perspective; they thereby encourage divisiveness and frustrate dialogue. The alternative to ideology is a cognitive style that narrows issues, bridges differences, and respects the complexity and variability of factual circumstances.[35]

More specifically, responsive law fosters civility in two basic ways:

1. *Overcoming the parochialism of communal morality.* The growing authority of purpose tends to attenuate both prescription and symbolism. Purposive law demands that custom and morality, insofar as they claim legal authority, be justified by a rational assessment of costs and benefits. One effect is pressure to decriminalize offenses against the prevailing moral code. The legal order is then "civilized," in the precise sense that it becomes more urbane, more receptive to cultural diversity, less prone to brutalize the deviant and the eccentric. It need not follow that law divorce itself from the moral consensus of the community. Rather, law finds consensus in general aspirations rather than in specific norms of conduct; it seeks to clarify the values at stake in the moral order, thus

32. Max Weber, "Politics as a Vocation," in H. H. Gerth and C. Wright Mills, eds., *From Max Weber: Essays in Sociology* (New York: Oxford University Press, 1958, 1946), p. 120ff.
33. Ibid., p. 121.
34. Ibid., p. 120.
35. This is the basic argument in Edward Shils' essay, "Ideology and Civility," reprinted in Shils, *The Intellectuals and the Powers and Other Essays*, p. 42.

purging the culture of its parochial elements. For example, the law may be loathe to criminalize rules regarding obscenity or pornography, but it may well take account of underlying values such as the protection of sexual experience from degradation or the maintenance of a civil diversity that provides areas insulated from assault on conventional life styles. In addressing these values, responsive law explores alternative means of achieving legal ends, especially noncriminal strategies of regulation such as zoning. In fact the search for alternatives to criminal prohibition may well enhance the law's capacity to fulfill its responsibility to the moral order.

2. *Encouraging a problem-centered and socially integrative approach to crises of public order.* During strikes, demonstrations, riots, or other crises of order, the routine assumptions of institutional life are challenged, and many rules of normal times are disregarded. In such settings, where the restoration of consensus is at stake, it is often unhelpful to insist on obedience to rules that are, in context, remote and irrelevant. A law that encourages criticism of rules, and even makes disobedience a legitimate means of testing and changing rules,[36] is better prepared to moderate struggles over symbolic threats to authority. Forgiveness for rule breaking is readily negotiated in the interest of reconstituting a framework within which cooperation can go forward.

The effect is to facilitate a quest for integrative resolutions of crises.[37] This posture assumes that the terms of public order are not rigidly fixed but, rather, open to renegotiation so that they will take better account of affected social interests. Hence,

36. Such a law recognizes certain kinds of disobedience as *civil*, whether or not it is morally justified. On this point see Bickel, *The Morality of Consent*, p. 91ff. The distinction between civil disobedience and conscientious objection is discussed in Hannah Arendt, *Crises of the Republic* (New York: Harcourt Brace Jovanovich, 1972), pp. 67–68.

37. The Western legal tradition, with its emphasis on determinate parties isolated from their social contexts and its preference for decisions that are

the *reconstruction* of social relations is taken to be a major resource for achieving public order. In other words, responsive law can more readily adopt a "political paradigm" in interpreting disobedience and disorder. That paradigm invokes a pluralistic model of the group structure of society, thus underlining the reality and affirming the legitimacy of social conflict. Disobedience may be seen as dissent, and deviance as the emergence of a new life style; riots are not dismissed as "senseless" or merely destructive mob actions but are appraised for their relevance as social protests. In this way the political—and civil—arts of negotiation, discussion, and compromise are brought into play.

In being sensitive to the political parameters of public order, responsive law shares a feature of repressive law; in this respect both contrast sharply with autonomous law. The latter, concerned with legal purity, keeps its distance from the political order and adheres to the rules without assuming responsibility for the consequences of enforcement. Repressive and responsive law are more interested in outcomes, and hence are more ready to deploy political resources. However, repressive law is fundamentally uncivil in its approach to power and to the group structure of society: It manipulates all sources of power, whether to seek alliance or quash opposition, in single-minded defense of a regime of domination. For example, maintaining order in a prison depends on a close understanding of the inmate social system, because warden and staff are heavily dependent on the collusion of key inmate leaders and must at the same time be prepared to destroy potential sources of

resolutely indifferent to social consequences, has lost confidence in recent years, with an attendant search for alternative models of dispute settlement. This may help account for the appeal of anthropological studies that celebrate modes of dispute settlement more fully attuned to the contexts of action and more committed to reestablishing relationships rather than sundering them. See Robert L. Kidder, "Afterword: Change and Structure in Dispute Processing," *Law and Society Review* **9** (1975): 385, 386–388.

recalcitrance.[38] This repressive instrumentalism differs sharply from the instrumentalism of responsive law. The latter is marked by purposive and civil regard for multiple ends and multiple interests.[39] In responsive law order is negotiated, not won by subordination.

The clashing perspectives of our three types of law were often vividly apparent in the handling of the riots and demonstrations of the 1960s. One set of complaints centered on repressive police tactics, for example, the *destruction* of crowds as distinguished from crowd control in the interest of peaceful public assembly.[40] Flagrantly repressive police practices were easily criticized and in principle controlled from the standpoint of the "rule of law." More difficult was a second set of problems, which arose from the failure of police to mobilize political resources. Acting as agents of autonomous law, the police could not readily entertain the idea that the restoration of order involved a duty to negotiate. In the Watts riots of 1965, for example, the police rebuffed efforts by community leaders to defuse the crisis.[41] There, the call for a more responsive and civil approach fell on deaf ears.

38. This pattern is discussed in Gresham M. Sykes, *The Society of Captives: A Study of a Maximum Security Prison* (Princeton, N.J.: Princeton University Press, 1958). See also Richard A. Cloward, "Social Control in the Prison," in Richard A. Cloward, Donald R. Cressey, George H. Grosser, Richard H. McCleery, Lloyd E. Ohlin, Gresham M. Sykes, and Sheldon L. Messinger, *Theoretical Studies in Social Organization of the Prison* (New York: Social Science Research Council, 1960), p. 20; Richard H. McCleery, "Communication Patterns as Bases of Systems of Authority and Power," in Cloward et al., p. 49; and Richard H. McCleery, "The Governmental Process and Informal Social Control," in Donald R. Cressey, ed., *The Prison: Studies in Institutional Organization and Change* (New York: Holt, Rinehart & Winston, 1961), p. 149.

39. See the discussion of instrumentation on pp. 82–86 and in note 18.

40. For a case study of police tactics of crowd destruction, see Rodney Stark, *Police Riots: Collective Violence and Law Enforcement* (Belmont, Ca.: Wadsworth, 1971), chap. 1.

41. See "Riot in Watts: Los Angeles, 1965," in Leonard Broom and Philip Selznick, *Sociology; A Text with Adapted Readings*, 6th ed. (New York: Harper & Row, 1977), pp. 234–238.

Legal and Political Participation

A corollary of attenuated obligation is a wider sharing of legal authority. As the legal system expands its critical resources, it delegates more discretion to decide what is authoritative. Legal participation takes on new meaning: Not only does it become less passive and less submissive; it also extends to the making and interpretation of legal policy.

In contrast, a rule-centered system concentrates authority. This is an attribute autonomous law shares with bureaucracy. In the rule-of-law model, the legal order is perceived as hierarchical and unitary. There is a close identification of law with state law, and of the state with a monolithic official hierarchy. The jurisprudential quest is for a theory of the legal system that will establish a clear chain of command and a precise locus of ultimate authority. With its emphasis on the "pedigree" of legal norms and on the ultimate subordination of law to the political sovereign, legal positivism neatly captures the ethos of autonomous law.

Conversely, contemporary criticism of the model of rules introduces, along with the theme of purpose, a strong pluralist motif. The accent—reminiscent of sociological jurisprudence —is on the multiplicity and diffuseness of the sources of law. This is a pervasive theme in the writings of Lon Fuller, who sees law as an emergent outcome of human interaction and objects to the positivist "tendency to convert every form of social ordering into an exercise of the authority of the state."[42] Plurality is most apparent where the law's primary role is to lend authority to private institutional arrangements, but it is also manifest in the widely diverse lawmaking mechanisms to be found within the framework of modern government.

42. Lon L. Fuller, "Mediation—Its Forms and Functions," *Southern California Law Review* **44** (1971): 305, 339.

One effect of legal pluralism is to multiply opportunities *within* the legal process for participation in the making of law. In this way the legal arena becomes a special kind of political forum[43] and legal participation takes on a political dimension. In other words, legal action comes to serve as a vehicle by which groups and organizations may participate in the determination of public policy. It is less exclusively perceived as a way of vindicating individual claims based on recognized rules.

The rise of social advocacy in the United States is one of the more remarkable features of recent legal history. Under the impetus of some private groups (notably the NAACP Legal Defense Fund) and the government itself (in the legal service programs of the Office of Economic Opportunity), we have seen a deliberate effort to make the legal process an alternative mode of political participation. The Supreme Court recognized this evolution as it upheld the right to organize for social advocacy:

In the context of NAACP objectives, litigation is not a technique for resolving private differences; it is a means for achieving the lawful objectives of equality of treatment by all government, federal, state and local, for the members of the Negro community in this country. It is thus a form of political expression.[44]

For the courts and for much of the legal profession, that evolution was fairly easy to accept. It gave effect to a well understood responsibility of the judicial branch for the protection of values and interests that are likely to be given short shrift in the politics of majority rule.[45]

43. This is a key theme of Stewart, pp. 1711–1760.
44. *NAACP* v. *Button*, 371 U.S. 415, 429 (1963). See also *Brotherhood of Railroad Trainmen* v. *Virginia*, 377 U.S. 1 (1964).
45. "[If] a special condition . . . tends seriously to curtail the operation of those political processes ordinarily relied upon to protect minorities, [it] may call for correspondingly more searching judicial inquiry." *U.S.* v. *Carolene Products*, 304 U.S. 144, 153 n. 4 (1938).

Social advocacy invokes legal authority and uses forums that can be held accountable to legal rules and principles. Hence, the characteristic locale of such advocacy is the court or the administrative agency rather than legislative bodies. The appeal is to legal entitlement, not to political will. Nevertheless, litigation is carried on with the express intent of furthering group interests and changing legal rules, including administrative policies. If a legal starting point is available— an argument founded in preexisting authority—advocacy can be used as a supplement to political action through legislative channels. This blending of legal and political participation encourages the assertion of new interests, but in a way that reaffirms the received values of the legal order. Even as political resources are deployed it remains understood that claims are subject to the test of legal authority and that the legal forum is one in which interest, will, and power are, in principle, never decisive by themselves.

The expansion of social advocacy contributes new points of view to legal debate and brings new bases of support to the development and implementation of public policy. When the right to counsel is extended, when class actions open the way for representation of social interests,[46] when "injury in fact" takes the place of formal entitlement as the criterion of standing,[47] the outcome is more than a broadening of access to legal institutions. Not less important is *an enlargement of the scope*

46. See, e.g., "Class Actions: A Study of Group Interest Litigation," *Race Relations Law Reporter* 1 (1965): 991. More generally, see "Developments in the Law—Class Actions," *Harvard Law Review* 89 (1976): 1318.

47. For developments in the law of standing see Kenneth C. Davis, "The Liberalized Law of Standing," *University of Chicago Law Review* 37 (1970): 450. But see Louis L. Jaffe, "Standing Again," *Harvard Law Review* 84 (1971): 633; and "The Citizen as Litigant in Public Actions: The Non-Hohfeldian or Ideological Plaintiff," *University of Pennsylvania Law Review* 116 (1968): 1033. See also Ernest Gellhorn, "Public Participation in Agency Proceedings," *Yale Law Journal* 81 (1972): 359; and Lee A. Albert, "Standing to Challenge Administrative Action: An Inadequate Surrogate for Claims for Relief," *Yale Law Journal* 83 (1974): 425.

of legal inquiry. What is at stake in the law of standing is, in part, the capacity of the legal order to inform itself of the range of issues and interests it affects—more generally, the ability to comprehend the group structure of society.[48] Furthermore, the inclusion of new constituencies brings added energy to the working of legal institutions. A policy of environmental protection gains vigor when regulatory agencies can count on active pro-ecology constituencies to generate complaints and mobilize influence, thus balancing the strength of industrial interests.[49] Regulation becomes more nearly "self-administering," less dependent on imposed official prescription.

Thus the enlargement of legal participation goes beyond increasing the democratic worth of the legal order. It can also contribute to the competence of legal institutions.[50] There is an instructive parallel in the effort of modern organizations to encourage participatory decision making.[51] The new administrative style borrows much from the experience (and the rhetoric) of democracy, but this is primarily a means to the

48. On interest representation as a "model" for administrative law see Stewart, esp. pp. 1760–1813.

49. See Joseph L. Sax, *Defending the Environment: A Strategy for Citizen Action* (New York: Knopf, 1971). This is also the central argument in Paul Sabatier, "Social Movements and Regulatory Agencies: Toward a More Adequate—and Less Pessimistic—Theory of 'Client Capture,' " *Policy Sciences* 6 (1975): 301. On the intervention of environmental groups before the AEC, see Steven Ebbin and Raphael Kaster, *Citizen Groups and the Nuclear Controversy* (Cambridge, Mass.: M.I.T. Press, 1974), and Daniel Bronstein, "The AEC Decision-Making Process and the Environment: A Case Study of the Calvert Cliffs Nuclear Power Plant," *Ecology Law Quarterly* 1 (1971): 689. On Sierra Club efforts to prevent the U.S. Forest Service from permitting development of the Mineral King Valley, see Christopher D. Stone, *Should Trees Have Standing? Toward Legal Rights for Natural Objects* (Los Altos, Ca.: William Kaufmann, 1974).

50. This is an assumption of the "interest representation model" of administrative law. Stewart, p. 1760.

51. For a suggestive treatment of this topic see Warren G. Bennis, *Changing Organizations* (New York: McGraw-Hill, 1966), and *Beyond Bureaucracy: Essays in the Development and Evolution of Human Organization* (New York: McGraw-Hill, 1973).

end of achieving a more purposive organization, free from the straitjacket of bureaucratic authority. The postbureaucratic organization is less preoccupied with administrative regularity. It presumes a context in which the value of rationality is firmly established[52] and the maintenance of official integrity is no longer at the top of the agenda. The special problem of postbureaucratic organization is to enlist participation, to encourage initiative and responsibility, to create what Barnard called "cooperative systems" capable of tapping the autonomous "contributions" of multiple constituents.[53] In purposive organization authority must be open and participatory: Consultation is encouraged; reasons for decisions are explained; criticism is welcome; consent is taken as a test of rationality.

The hallmarks of postbureaucratic organization are the following:

1. Broad delegations of authority to mobilize and deploy resources for the achievement of set goals. Decentralization replaces "edict management,"[54] but decentralization is not understood as the establishment of subordinate "jurisdictions." The model is the task force organization made up of temporary problem-centered units.

2. Creative use of planning, evaluation, and development staffs to increase the cognitive competence of the organization. A corollary is that staff and line must learn to share authority.

52. By contrast, bureaucracy, as Weber understood it, is mainly a way of protecting decision making from sources of arbitrariness; hence, it presumes a context in which the value of rationality is still precarious. See p. 64.
53. Chester I. Barnard, *The Functions of the Executive* (Cambridge, Mass.: Harvard University Press, 1968, 1938), esp. pp. 65–81. Barnard insisted that an organization must be conceived to "include all actions of contributions and receipt of energies, so that a customer making a purchase, a supplier furnishing supplies, an investor furnishing capital, are also contributors." (p. 77).
54. Peter F. Drucker, *Concept of the Corporation* (Boston: Beacon Press, 1960, 1946), p. 48, and more generally pp. 41–71.

3. Acceptance of dual supervision and dual loyalty in order to encourage the independence of judgment that comes, for example, when organizational participation is qualified by professional commitments and aspirations.

4. Participatory decision making as a source of knowledge, a vehicle of communication, and a foundation for consent.

These principles and forms are "the leaven in the bureaucratic dough."[55]

Following a similar logic, a purposive legal order may require a relaxation of central authority in the interest of more effective cooperative action. Even in the Soviet Union some movement in that direction has been observed. As purpose becomes more central, notes Golunskii,[56] "the significance of state compulsion as a means of securing the realization of norms of socialist law is steadily diminishing." A centralized, rule-centered law is expedient when "one is dealing with typical, recurring situations, that will be repeated also in the future." But "when a new task is placed before society, when it is necessary to organize people for carrying out activity which has never been carried out before, and which in the future, when analogous tasks arise, will not be a simple repetition of what was done earlier . . . it becomes more difficult to prescribe directly from the center the concrete actions that must be or need not be taken to accomplish each of the multiple and variegated tasks." The law must then proceed through "a whole series of assignments to various state agencies," leaving them "with a significantly broader area for showing their initiative in selecting ways and means," emphasizing their "active organizational role" and their responsibility to enlist

55. Broom and Selznick, p. 209.
56. The following quotes are from S. A. Golunskii, "On the Question of the Concept of Legal Norms," *Sovetskoe Gosudarstvo i Pravo (Soviet State and Law)* (1961), no. 4: 21, trans. by Harold J. Berman (unpublished course material for Comparison of Soviet and American Law, Harvard Law School).

"the participation of the public in the realization of legal norms."

But civic participation can undermine as well as support institutional efficacy. Sustained participation depends on the work of committed elites. As a result there is always a risk that more articulate constituencies will drown out weaker, less visible, or more passive publics. Policy is attenuated and regulation weakened when industrial power meets no effective challenge from the unorganized mass of consumers;[57] when decentralization and "grass roots" participation mean that powerful local interests overshadow wider but more remote interests;[58] when specialization results in narrowing administrative constituencies, so that other related interests are neglected;[59] when active participants are divorced from the

---

57. This is a main theme in the Study Group Reports issued by the Center for the Study of Responsive Law. See, e.g., Robert C. Fellmeth, *The Interstate Commerce Commission: The Public Interest and the ICC* (New York: Grossman, 1970); John C. Esposito, *Vanishing Air* (New York: Grossman, 1970); James S. Turner, *The Chemical Feast* (New York: Grossman, 1971); Mark J. Green, with Beverly C. Moore, Jr. and Bruce Wasserstein, *The Closed Enterprise System* (New York: Grossman, 1972); Mark J. Green, ed., *The Monopoly Makers* (New York: Grossman, 1973).

58. See Grant McConnell, *Private Power and American Democracy* (New York: Knopf, 1966). See also Philip Selznick, *TVA and the Grass Roots* (Berkeley: University of California Press, 1949); Sidney Baldwin, *Poverty and Politics: The Rise and Decline of the Farm Security Administration* (Chapel Hill, N.C.: University of North Carolina Press, 1968); Arthur Maass, "Congress and Water Resources," *American Political Science Review* **44** (1950): 576, and *The Kings River Project* (New York: Harcourt Brace Jovanovich, 1952).

59. This is a common focus of criticism in studies dealing with the "professionalization" or "bureaucratization" of institutions dispensing welfare, education, medical care, etc. On schools, see, e.g., David Rogers, *110 Livingston Street* (New York: Random House, 1968); Marilyn Gittell et al., *School Boards and School Policy: An Evaluation of Decentralization in New York City* (New York: Praeger, 1973). On Welfare, see Peter Marris and Martin Rein, *Dilemmas of Social Reform: Poverty and Community Action in the United States* (New York: Atherton Press, 1967). On hospitals, see Charles Perrow, "Hospitals: Technology, Goals, and Structure," in James G. March, ed., *Handbook of Organizations* (Chicago: Rand-McNally, 1965), p. 910.

groups they represent, and when the claims they press distort the needs for which they speak.[60]

In these and similar ways the enlargement of participation makes the definition and protection of the public interest precarious and problematic. As institutions are opened to their constituencies, they become (1) more vulnerable to the imbalances of power in society and (2) more readily focused on a narrow range of special concerns. They become, in effect, less accountable to the larger polity, more tenuously informed by its problems and aspirations.[61]

Thus the diffusion of legal authority and the enlargement of legal participation bring about a "withering away of the state."[62] Paradoxically, the administrative explosion of modern

60. See the discussion of the problems inherent in "public interest" representation in Stewart, pp. 1762–1770. See also Philippe Nonet, *Administrative Justice: Advocacy and Change in a Government Agency* (New York: Russell Sage Foundation, 1969), pp. 96–97, 120–121; 261–267; Edgar S. Cahn and Jean C. Cahn, "Power to the People or the Profession? The Public Interest in Public Interest Law," *Yale Law Journal* **79** (1970): 1005; Harry Brill, "The Uses and Abuses of Legal Assistance," *Public Interest* **31** (1973): 38.

61. "Nor are laws right which are passed for the good of particular classes and not for the good of the whole state. States which have such laws are not polities but parties, and their notion of justice is simply unmeaning." Plato, *Laws*, Book IV, par. 715, in *Dialogues*, transl. by Benjamin Jowett (New York: Oxford University Press, 1892). Some recent political theory suggests that "participatory democracy" can cure the ills of pluralism. For example, Carole Pateman, *Participation and Democratic Theory* (Cambridge: Cambridge University Press, 1970). Social advocacy is a form of participatory democracy in that it offers alternative channels of political action outside the framework of majoritarian democracy on behalf of the socially disprivileged and on behalf of vulnerable values such as environmental protection. This kind of participation offsets the restrictive effects of "establishment" pluralism, in which a relatively closed circle of governing elites and complacent institutions dominates the political process. By itself, however, this enlargement of participation only widens the circle. The basic problems of pluralism remain.

62. This phrase first appeared in Lenin's comments on Marx's *Critique of the Gotha Programme*, published in *The State and Revolution*. A con-

times has blurred and weakened the conception of the state as a single, undifferentiated agency of public power. A new model of the legal and political system is suggested by the emergence of a "fourth branch" of government, reflecting many of the aspirations and problems of a purposive and responsive law. In that model legal authority is widely delegated; special-purpose institutions, of all kinds and in large numbers, are the critical bearers of legal responsibility and the sources of growth in law; they are endowed with broad discretionary powers and are less concerned with prescribing conduct than with enlisting cooperation; each works in close relation with its own constituencies. In such a context the symbolism of Sovereignty is weakened and gives way to the image of a loose aggregate of Public Corporations, each with its own mission and its own public. A sober look at this image reveals the risks as well as the promise of pluralism. There is the spectre of a multitude of narrow-ended, self-regulating institutions, working at cross-purposes and bound to special interests; of a system impervious to direction and leadership, incapable of setting priorities; of a fragmented and impotent polity in which the very idea of public interest is emptied of meaning.[63]

---

venient source is Karl Marx, *Critique of the Gotha Programme, with Appendices by Marx, Engels, and Lenin* (New York: International Publishers, 1966), pp. 55, 67–88. The idea need not be understood as suggesting the end of all government; it should be interpreted as pointing to a transformation of government away from monolithic and repressive forms of the state.

63. The dilution of public interest in pluralism is criticized in Lowi, *The End of Liberalism* (New York: W. W. Norton & Co., 1969); McConnell, *Private Power and American Democracy*; Nonet, "Taking Purpose Seriously." For an extreme statement of the pluralist doctrine that the "public interest" has no objective content, see Glendon A. Schubert, Jr., " 'The Public Interest' in Administrative Decision-Making," *American Political Science Review* **51** (1957): 346. See also the writings of Charles Lindblom cited in note 20. As Stewart points out, similar views are implicit in the "interest representation model" of administrative law. Stewart, p. 1712.

From Fairness to Competence

We have seen that purposive law is most clearly manifest in a sharpening of legal criticism. Legal criticism, in turn, makes legal obligation problematic and negotiable, vulnerable to discretionary judgment and hence to the pressures of the social and political environment. The outcome is a regime of legal pluralism that has both the virtues and the vices of openness. As we argued earlier, openness is a necessary but not sufficient condition of responsiveness. By itself, openness undermines the integrity and competence of legal institutions. If the legal order is to be responsive and not merely opportunistic, its institutions need effective tutelage in the accommodation of pressure. In other words, purpose must gain affirmative as well as critical authority. This is the most problematic aspect of the quest for responsive law, and the one requiring the most radical break from the perspectives of autonomous law.

Legitimacy, not competence, is the central concern of autonomous law. At that stage the main business of law is to certify the authority of rules and decisions, and not to ensure that institutions have the will and the competence to carry out their mandates. Hence, the paradigmatic function of the legal order is adjudication rather than policy making or administration. Policy issues arise in adjudication, but only incidentally, more out of logical necessity than out of direct responsibility. Autonomous law is court-centered, and its constitutional arrangements ensure that the courts remain "the least dangerous branch," the branch least competent to assemble and deploy resources, institute systematic changes in policy and practice, or address the problems involved in getting things done. The court's commitment is to hearing claims; its expertise lies in procedural fairness; its contribution is to restrain authority and vindicate individual rights. In none of these ways can law address the problem of making purpose effective in guiding institutions.

This limitation of autonomous law has become apparent in the recent history of judicial activism in the United States. Under the leadership of the Warren Court, and spurred by an explosion of social advocacy, the courts extended the scope of judicial review to wider domains of public policy. But characteristically their emphasis remained on challenge and legitimation. Procedural reform—multiplying opportunities for the assertion of claims—was the thrust of judicial intervention, with little testing of substantive benefits[64] and little regard for costs, including the burdens imposed on party initiative.[65] Individual rights—for example, the rights of voters or criminal defendants—remained the starting point of legal analysis, with only incidental attention to institutional outcomes—for example, the transformation of the electoral system or the reform of bail.[66] And judicial remedies were geared to the case at hand rather than to the patterns or practices out of which cases arose.[67] When the courts sought to transcend these limitations

64. See, e.g., the evidence on the impact of the Supreme Court's decision *In re Gault*. William V. Stapleton and Lee E. Teitelbaum, *In Defense of Youth; A Study of the Role of Counsel in American Juvenile Courts* (New York: Russell Sage Foundation, 1972).

65. On the costs associated with the expansion of procedural remedies, see Stewart, pp. 1770–1776. See also Nonet, *Administrative Justice*, pp. 125–159, 234–240; Joel Handler, "Controlling Official Behavior in Welfare Administration," *California Law Review* **54** (1966): 479; and Richard M. Titmuss, "Welfare Rights, Law and Discretion," *Political Quarterly* **42** (1971): 113.

66. On voting, see Bickel, *Politics and the Warren Court*, pp. 175–198; and *The Supreme Court and the Idea of Progress*. On bail reform, see Forrest Dill, *Bail and Bail Reform in the United States*, unpublished doctoral dissertation, University of California, Berkeley, 1971.

67. That is why, as Jaffe argues, "the work done by public actions could . . . be *better* performed in most—though possibly not in all—cases by political and administrative controls." Louis L. Jaffe, *Judicial Control of Administrative Action* (Boston: Little, Brown, 1965), p. 476. Even the "exclusionary rule," a device explicitly intended to change patterns of law

and to address institutional problems more directly—for example, in school desegregation cases—they did so at the peril of legal and political overreaching.[68]

Social advocacy and judicial activism stretch the limits of the rule-of-law model but signal no alternative to it.[69] If the legal order is to lend affirmative authority to purpose, the focus of legal analysis must be the social patterns and institutional arrangements that frustrate the achievement of legal ends, not the aggrieved individual per se. In the context of responsive law, claims of right are understood as opportunities for uncovering disorder or malfunction, and hence may be valued as administrative resources. But the resolution of controversies cannot remain the paradigmatic concern, nor can law depend on that process to fulfill its responsibilities. Procedural justice is only one obligation among others and one resource among others. It does not follow that fairness and individual justice are valued any less. On the contrary, purposive law encourages a fuller realization that individual justice, in the long run and not only in the case at hand, depends on supportive institutional conditions. Legal energies should be devoted to diagnosing institutional problems and redesigning institutional

---

enforcement behavior, has apparently had little impact on systematic evasion of constitutional standards. See Dallin H. Oaks, "Studying the Exclusionary Rule in Search and Seizure," *University of Chicago Law Review* 37 (1970): 665.

68. On judicial overreaching in school desegregation see Philip B. Kurland, *The Quality of Inequality: Urban and Suburban Public Schools* (Chicago: University of Chicago Press, 1968), pp. 60–67; and *Politics, the Constitution, and the Warren Court* (Chicago: University of Chicago Press, 1970), pp. 105–113, 195–206. See also Nathan Glazer, "Towards an Imperial Judiciary?" and "Is Busing Necessary?" *Commentary*, March 1972, p. 39; David Kirp, "School Desegregation and the Limits of Legalism," *Public Interest*, Spring 1977, p. 101; and Joan C. Baratz, "Court Decisions and Educational Change: A Case History of the D.C. Public Schools, 1954–1974," *Journal of Law and Education* 4 (1975): 63.

69. The limits of social advocacy in such contexts as welfare and housing are discussed in Peter Miller, *Social Advocacy and the Legal Process*, unpublished doctoral dissertation, University of California, Berkeley, 1974.

arrangements. New modes of supervision, new ways of increasing the visibility of decisions, new organizational units, new structures of authority, new incentives—these are the characteristic remedies of purposive law.[70]

A basic principle is that the burden of correcting unlawfulness or injustice should not fall on the individual claimant; rather, legal institutions should be capable of correcting themselves. Thus it may be that, in a particular context, procedural changes granting larger due process rights to potential claimants are in order; but this conclusion should not follow from a predisposition to rely on formal procedures for curing substantive harms. Rather, it should be the outcome of a diagnostic inquiry that (1) finds a pervasive lack of fairness rather than an isolated instance and (2) justifies the expectation that a change of administrative routine—for example, a provision for notice or hearing or appeal—will cure the problem. For by itself an isolated case would hardly justify the conclusion that an institutional change is necessary; it might not warrant more than a *de minimis* expression of regret. And if the unfairness is pervasive it may well be the result of institutional flaws—ignorance, lack of resources, conflicting pressures—that no procedural rule can cure.[71] In fact, as we have emphasized, formal accountability can suffocate institutions, paralyze energies, and hinder problem solving, thus aggravating instead of controlling incompetence.[72]

The "master ideal" of responsive law, as of autonomous law, is legality. That continuity remains. But the ideal of legality should not be confused with the paraphernalia of

---

70. An illustration of this approach, in the context of the modern corporation, is Christopher D. Stone, *Where the Law Ends: The Social Control of Corporate Behavior* (New York: Harper & Row, 1975); and "The Corporate Fix," *The Center Magazine* 9 (July–August 1976): 15–22.
71. On the limited worth of procedural change see notes 64–67.
72. See pp. 60–65.

"legalization"[73]—the proliferation of rules and procedural formalities. The bureaucratic patterns that pass for due process (understood as an "obstacle course"[74]) or for accountability (understood as compliance with official rules) are alien to responsive law. The ideal of legality needs to be conceived more generally and to be cured of formalism. In a purposive system legality is the progressive reduction of arbitrariness in positive law and its administration.[75] To press for a maximum feasible reduction of arbitrariness is to demand a system of law that is capable of reaching beyond formal regularity and procedural fairness to substantive justice. That achievement, in turn, requires institutions that are competent as well as legitimate.

If there is a paradigmatic function of responsive law, it is regulation, not adjudication.[76] Broadly understood, regulation is the process of elaborating and correcting the policies re-

73. "Legalization," and the institutional pathologies associated with it, are the central theme of Nonet, *Administrative Justice*, esp. pp. 125–268. More generally, Fuller argues that human institutions are paralyzed by the "creeping legalism" that follows from reliance on rules, because "legal rules are not an effective device for directing human energies to those places where they can be most creatively and effectively applied." Lon L. Fuller, "Two Principles of Human Association," in J. Roland Pennock and John W. Chapman, eds., *Voluntary Associations* (New York: Atherton Press, 1969), pp. 13–14. See also Judith N. Shklar, *Legalism* (Cambridge, Mass.: Harvard University Press, 1964).

74. Herbert L. Packer, "Two Models of the Criminal Process," *University of Pennsylvania Law Review* **113** (1964): 1, 13.

75. This formulation of the ideal of legality was first proposed in Philip Selznick, "Sociology and Natural Law," *Natural Law Forum* **6** (1961): 84, 100.

76. Abram Chayes makes much the same point in analyzing the "new model" of "public law litigation" that he sees emerging in the federal trial courts. Chayes, "The Role of the Judge in Public Law Litigation," *Harvard Law Review* **89** (1976): 1281. In the new model "the subject matter of the law suit is not a dispute between private individuals about private rights, but a grievance about the operation of public policy . . . Just as the traditional concept reflected and related to a system in which social and economic arrangements were remitted to autonomous private action, so the new model reflects and relates to a regulatory system where these arrangements are the product of positive enactment. In such a system, enforce-

quired for the realization of a legal purpose. Regulation thus conceived is a mechanism for clarifying the public interest. It involves testing alternative strategies for the implementation of mandates and reconstructing those mandates in the light of what is learned. This function cannot be identified with the work of "regulatory agencies" as we know them. Rule making and enforcement may be involved in the regulatory function, but they do not define it—that is, unless they are understood in the far larger sense of policy making and administration. Making "rules," *sensu stricto*, is only one way among many of elaborating policy, for example, establishing "performance criteria," defining "operational goals," formulating "guidelines." And prescribing is only one of many ways of getting things done, for example, allocating resources, creating incentives, establishing facilities, providing services. In the perspective of autonomous law, agencies like the Corps of Engineers, the U.S. Employment Service, or a public school system are not readily conceived as part of the "legal process"; and yet the basic decisions by which they define their missions and strategies involve them in the performance of a regulatory function. To exclude that reality from the legal process is to (1) deprive the "nonlegal" institutions of government from the benefit of law's expertise in the practical and intellectual art of setting standards and (2) deprive "legal" agencies of "nonlegal" resources, thus confining them to a constricting, sometimes crippling model of "regulation through legal orders."[77]

---

ment and application of law is necessarily implementation of regulatory policy" (pp. 1302, 1304). One may, as Chayes does, raise questions about the competence of courts to fulfill that function. Chayes, pp. 1307–1309.

77. Bruce Ackerman et al., *The Uncertain Search for Environmental Quality* (New York: Free Press, 1974), p. 221ff. Notice also Jaffe's thesis that many weaknesses of regulatory agencies result from the separation of regulation from management. Louis L. Jaffe, "The Effective Limits of the Administrative Process: A Reevaluation," *Harvard Law Review* **67** (1954): 1105.

Purposive regulation presumes a far wider and inclusive conception of the legal process. In that perspective law is a problem-solving, facilitative enterprise that can bring to bear a variety of powers and mobilize an array of intellectual and organizational resources. This was the thrust of the legal realist plea for an integrative vision of "law-government."[78] Any theory that makes problem solving a central function of law readily appreciates that the barriers by which institutions are separated, "spheres of competence" defined, and bureaucratic turfs enclosed hinder the deployment of resources necessary for effective action. This is why a responsive legal order must postulate that "the danger of tyranny or injustice lurks in unchecked power, not in blended power."[79] In other words, and more generally, the risks of arbitrariness in the exercise of power should be controlled in ways that facilitate, rather than hinder, the enlargement of institutional competence. For in proportion as the law assumes ever wider responsibilities incompetence becomes an ever more lively source of arbitrary power.

A corollary of the blending of powers is a further attenuation of "distinctively legal" institutions, ideas, and modes of reasoning. We have already pointed to several aspects of this evolution: With purposive law there is a decline of artificial reason, a convergence of legal and policy analysis, a reintegration of legal and moral judgment and of legal and political participation.[80] Another facet of that transformation is the absorption of law into the larger realm of administration. The lawyerly art becomes the art of giving affirmative authority to purpose, that is, of ensuring that purpose is taken seriously in the working and deliberations of legal-governmental institutions.

78. Karl N. Llewellyn, *Jurisprudence; Realism in Theory and Practice* (Chicago: University of Chicago Press, 1962), p. 357ff.
79. Kenneth C. Davis, *Administrative Law Text* (St. Paul, Minn.: West Publishing, 1959), p. 30.
80. See pp. 82–83, 89, 96–97.

And that depends, to a large extent, on organizational dynamics. The key function of administrative leadership is "the institutional embodiment of purpose."[81] Policy must be built into the social structure of the enterprise so that it informs decision making at all levels and hence attains effective, in-depth authority. Such a condition is widely coveted but not easily attained. It requires creating subunits with special skills and commitments, distributing authority so that critical decisions are made where purpose is best understood, and managing incentives so that energies are enlisted and initiative is released.

This argument is more than a reaffirmation of the centrality of administrative law in the modern legal order. Administrative law as we know it is better understood as an heir of autonomous law than as a harbinger of responsive law. It remains a law of the judicial review of administrative actions, a law of the procedural rights of parties affected by administrative decisions, a law of the grounds for invalidating administrative policies and restraining administrative powers. Responsive law aims at *enablement and facilitation*; restrictive accountability is a secondary function. A new kind of lawyerly expertise is envisioned—expertise in the articulation of *principles of institutional design and institutional diagnosis*. Such principles would analyze the characteristic institutional problems that are associated with carrying out different kinds of mandates and exercising different kinds of powers in different kinds of environments, and would point to the institutional mechanisms by which such problems may be corrected or moderated. The long term goal would be a capacity "to determine the most harmonious fit between the purposes and characteristics of particular agencies and various control techniques."[82] Developing such principles will require a close analysis of adminis-

---

81. Philip Selznick, *Leadership in Administration: A Sociological Interpretation* (New York: Harper & Row, 1957), pp. 62–63, 90–133.
82. Stewart, p. 1810.

trative experience, to clarify, for example, what conditions help increase cognitive competence, including the effective use of policy and planning staffs; what modes of decentralization are consistent with preserving the integrity of programs; what kinds of negotiation further or undermine vigorous enforcement;[83] more generally, what blend of cognitive, organizational, and political resources specific types of agencies require for the realization of their distinctive purposes.[84]

Although responsive law envisions a blending of powers and a blurring of institutional boundaries, the distinction between legal and political decisions is not erased. On the contrary, a legal process that aims at enlarging the competence of legal institutions presumes that (1) institutional design and evaluation may build upon *received* premises fixing the ends law is to serve and (2) the legal task is to reduce arbitrariness in the definition and elaboration of these ends. The union of law and government means, in effect, that in responsive law government acts in a dual capacity. As a *political* actor it assumes responsibility for deciding what ends are to be pursued and what resources it is prepared to commit in dealing with problems such as pollution control or discrimination in employment. These decisions express and impose a political will, and they properly reflect the play of political power, however restrained and sublimated it may be. But government must then proceed, as a *legal* actor, to establish the agencies and mechanisms by which public ends will be furthered. In principle, though with only limited success in practice, these institutions are designed to bring maximum objectivity to the elaboration of public policy, including more precise definition of received purposes and progressive clarification of political

83. For a case study of this problem see Alfred W. Blumrosen, "The Crossroads for Equal Employment Opportunity: Incisive Administration or Indecisive Bureaucracy," *Notre Dame Lawyer* **49** (1973): 46.

84. Compare Stewart's conclusion that comparative analysis is the "line of inquiry that may represent our best hope of realistic future progress in administrative law." Stewart, p. 1810.

choices and strategic options. Given certain contexts and resources, by what responsible and operational goals may policy be governed? What alternative ends, within the framework of a basic mandate, would be warranted by other ways of allocating resources? What resources does a given purpose truly require? In that legal capacity government transcends power politics. It looks beyond the demands made on it to the needs it must meet, reaches out to powerless interests, elicits participation, takes initiative to discover emerging problems and inchoate aspirations.

Accordingly, although there is a potential for responsiveness in any developed legal order, the fulfillment of that promise depends on a supportive political context. Responsive law presupposes a society that has the political capacity to face its problems, establish its priorities, and make the necessary commitments. For responsive law is no maker of miracles in the realm of justice. Its achievements depend on the will and resources of the political community.[85] Its distinctive contribution is to facilitate public purpose and build a spirit of self-correction into the governmental process.

85. As are the achievements of regulatory and other government agencies. The study of administrative experience has generated considerable skepticism about the competence of government agencies. In our view this skepticism is overdone and based on a superficial reading of the evidence. In the evaluation of public institutions it is necessary to distinguish more sharply between weaknesses that follow from the very mandate and resources of an agency and other weaknesses that stem more directly from the inner dynamics of institutional experience. Agencies are too easily criticized for "failing" to achieve mandates or to exercise powers they never received. No reasonable reading of their mandates warrants the sweeping conclusion that "regulatory and other government bodies [are] charged with protecting the public from corporate greed and irresponsibility"; yet this is the standard on which Nader bases his indictments. Ralph Nader, ed., *The Consumer and Corporate Accountability* (New York: Harcourt Brace Jovanovich, 1973), p. 215. More caution is needed, especially when, as in the American system, the political vulnerability of administrative agencies is acute. On this point see Harold Seidman, *Power, Position, and Politics* (New York: Oxford University Press, 1970), pp. 36–97. See also Louis Jaffe, "The Illusion of the Ideal Administration," *Harvard Law Review* **86** (1973): 1183, 1188–1199.

Epilogue:

Two Ways Law Can Die

The most general aim of this essay has been to restate the message of legal realism and sociological jurisprudence. Those doctrines were framed as a call for more empirical study of law. But that intellectual lesson, by itself hardly debatable, disguised an agenda of reform. *Responsive law, not sociology, was the true program of sociological and realist jurisprudence.* The problems they addressed—the limits of formalism, the enlargement of legal knowledge, the role of policy in legal judgment—presumed a legal order that would undertake an affirmative responsibility for the problems of society. That vision makes special sense in modern conditions, but it is nonetheless bound to a specific historical context. Impatient with all they found anachronistic in law, the jurisprudential advocates of sociological awareness were for the most part unable to appreciate the diversity of legal experience.[1] We have sought to place responsive law in a larger framework by delineating alternative models of law and society, each with its

---

1. Clearly Roscoe Pound must be excepted from this characterization. He was sharply conscious of the continuity between "sociological jurisprudence" and the "socialization of law." Pound, I, 347–358; 429–432; 526–547.

own problems and aspirations. Our approach stresses the continuing relevance of repressive and autonomous law even in contemporary society. At the same time, it revises and enlarges the agenda for sociolegal research.

In conclusion, it may be helpful to restate the main point of the developmental model we have proposed, that is, the sense in which responsive law represents a "higher" stage of legal evolution than autonomous and repressive law. Our thesis is that responsive law brings larger institutional competencies to the quest for justice. This evaluation, however, does not entail an unambiguous prescription or counsel. In our view responsive law is a precarious ideal whose achievement *and desirability* are historically contingent and depend especially on the urgencies to be met and the resources that can be tapped. Where maintaining order or taming repression require all available energies, a call for responsive law can only be a harmful distraction from more basic urgencies. Even where opportunities are present, the desirability of greater responsiveness may depend on how far a society or an institution should go in sacrificing other values, such as the achievement of high culture, to the quest for justice.[2]

To those who may, in view of these considerations, find the imagery of "development" misleading, the model can be recast as pointing to two ways law can die, that is, lose its distinctive identity. Historically, the idea of law has been intimately associated with the particular ideals, thoughtways, and institutional paraphernalia of the rule-of-law model. That is indeed the stage at which the legal order differentiates itself most sharply from the environing social and political order,

---

2. The conflicting demands of justice and other values, though not sufficiently well understood, present societies with critical choices. Recall Tocqueville's admonition that one of the prices justice exacts is mediocrity. Alexis de Tocqueville, *Democracy in America* (New York: Schocken Books, 1961), I, 296.

and can most readily claim a special expertise and a distinctive responsibility. Integrity and insularity sustain each other and account for the highly manifest and remarkably stable achievements of autonomous law.

In both its repressive and its responsive modes, the legal order loses the protection of firm institutional boundaries and becomes an integral part of government and politics. Hence, there is an attenuation of "distinctively legal" ideas and modes of thought. The death of law, in that sense, is a mark of both stages.[3] In both repressive and responsive law the authority of rules is weakened; discretion is enlarged; an instrumental perspective undermines the formalism of "artificial reason"; legal argument is less easily distinguishable from policy analysis; and legal institutions become at once more accessible and more vulnerable. These conditions create a risk of regression from responsiveness to repression.

Nevertheless, despite an apparent convergence, there is a moral gulf between repressive and responsive law. In repression, the integration of law and politics abridges the civilizing values of the rule of law, that is, legality conceived as fairness and restraint in the use of power. In a responsive legal order, the reintegration of law and government is a way of enlarging the meaning and reach of legal values from a set of minimal restrictions to a source of affirmative responsibilities. There is much risk in that enterprise, for law cannot extend its authority without also giving up at least some of its earlier, well-tested institutional defenses. But there is also the possibility that the legal order can make up for that loss by more effectively tapping the resources of the social order. In ministering to legal values, responsive law leans upon and preserves a

---

3. The "death of law" as a distinctive institutional system does not mean that, from an analytical standpoint, legal phenomena, as defined on pp. 10–13, no longer exist. This definition makes no assumption about institutional forms.

political community that is inclusive, not the property of a few, and a social organization that is rich in mechanisms for recalling government to its basic purposes. Although no longer bound to earlier institutional forms, the distinction between law and politics can nevertheless be retained.[4] Now indeed it has a larger import and more substantive aims: to reduce the elements of expediency and particularism in the political process, to distill the enduring moral commitments that emerge from political decisions, and to develop a theory of the public interest that can enhance the rationality of political discourse and moderate the self-serving use of power in political conflict. Put another way, the fundamental difference between repressive and responsive law is what separates "power politics," the raw conflict and accommodation of special interests, from "high politics," the reasoned effort to realize an ideal of polity.

4. See also pp. 112–113.

Index